First World War
and Army of Occupation
War Diary
France, Belgium and Germany

39 DIVISION
Divisional Troops
228 Machine Gun Company
2 September 1914 - 28 February 1918

WO95/2577/5

The Naval & Military Press Ltd
www.nmarchive.com
Published in association with The National Archives

Published by

The Naval & Military Press Ltd

Unit 10 Ridgewood Industrial Park,

Uckfield, East Sussex,

TN22 5QE England

Tel: +44 (0) 1825 749494

www.naval-military-press.com

www.nmarchive.com

This diary has been reprinted in facsimile from the original. Any imperfections are inevitably reproduced and the quality may fall short of modern type and cartographic standards.

© **Crown Copyright**
Images reproduced by permission of The National Archives, London, England, 2015.

Contents

Document type	Place/Title	Date From	Date To
Heading	WO95/2577/5		
Heading	228th Machine Gun Coy. Jly 1917-Dec 1917.		
Miscellaneous			
Heading	War Diary Of From 12th July 1917 To 31st July 1917. Volume 1		
Heading			
War Diary	Le Havre	12/07/1917	16/07/1917
Miscellaneous			
War Diary	Le Havre	17/07/1917	19/07/1917
Miscellaneous			
War Diary	Poperinge Area	20/07/1917	22/07/1917
Miscellaneous			
War Diary	Hilltop Sector	22/07/1917	24/07/1917
Miscellaneous			
War Diary	Hilltop Sector Refce Map St Julien 28 NW.2 1/10,000	24/07/1917	25/07/1917
Miscellaneous			
War Diary	Hilltop Sector Ref Map St Julien 28 NW 2 1/10,000	25/07/1917	26/07/1917
Miscellaneous			
War Diary	Hilltop Sector Ref Map St Julien 28 NW 2 1/10,000	26/07/1917	27/07/1917
Miscellaneous			
War Diary	Hilltop Sector Ref Map St. Julien 28 NW 2 1/10,000	28/07/1917	28/07/1917
Miscellaneous			
War Diary	Hilltop Sector Ref. Map St. Julien 28 NW 2 1/10,000	29/07/1917	29/07/1917
Miscellaneous			
War Diary	Hilltop Sector Ref Map St. Julien 28 NW 2 1/10,000	30/07/1917	31/07/1917
Miscellaneous			
War Diary	Hill Top Sector Ref Map St Julien 28 NW 2 1/10,000	31/07/1917	31/07/1917
Miscellaneous			
War Diary	N. of Ypres Hill Top Sector map Ref. St Julien 28 NW 2 1/10000	01/08/1917	01/08/1917
Miscellaneous			
War Diary	N. of Ypres Hill Top Sector Map Ref St Julien 28 NW 2 1/10,000	01/08/1917	02/08/1917
Miscellaneous			
War Diary	N. of Ypres Hilltop Sector map Refce St. Julien 28 NW 2 1/10000	02/08/1917	03/08/1917
Miscellaneous			
War Diary	N. of Ypres Hill Top Sector map Refce St Julien 28 NW 2 1/10,000	04/08/1917	05/08/1917
Miscellaneous			
War Diary	Canal Bank Hill Top Sector	06/08/1917	07/08/1917
War Diary	Piebrouch	08/08/1917	08/08/1917
Miscellaneous			
War Diary	Piebrouck map Refce R27a39 Belgium 4 France Sheet 27 1/40,000	09/08/1917	12/08/1917
Miscellaneous			
War Diary		12/08/1917	13/08/1917
Miscellaneous			
War Diary	Ridge Wood N.5c 10.97 France 28 SW 1/20,000	14/08/1917	14/08/1917
Miscellaneous			

War Diary Miscellaneous	Hollebeke Sector	14/08/1917	14/08/1917
War Diary Miscellaneous	Hollebeke Sector	14/08/1917	15/08/1917
War Diary Miscellaneous		15/08/1917	16/08/1917
War Diary Miscellaneous	Hollebeke Sector	16/08/1917	17/08/1917
War Diary Miscellaneous	Hollebeke Sector	17/08/1917	19/08/1917
War Diary Miscellaneous	Hollebeke Sector	19/08/1917	20/08/1917
War Diary Miscellaneous	Hollebeke Sector	20/08/1917	20/08/1917
War Diary Miscellaneous	Hollebeke Sector	21/08/1917	22/08/1917
War Diary Miscellaneous	Hollebeke Sector	23/08/1917	24/08/1917
War Diary Miscellaneous	Hollebeke Sector	25/08/1917	27/08/1917
War Diary Miscellaneous	Hollebeke Sector	26/08/1917	27/08/1917
War Diary Miscellaneous	Hollebeke Sector	28/08/1917	29/08/1917
War Diary Miscellaneous	Hollebeke Sector	29/08/1917	30/08/1917
War Diary Miscellaneous	Hollebeke Sector	30/08/1917	31/08/1917
War Diary Miscellaneous	Hollebeke Sector	01/09/1917	02/09/1917
War Diary Miscellaneous	Hollebeke Sector	02/09/1914	02/09/1914
War Diary	Hollebeke Sector	03/09/1914	03/09/1914
War Diary Miscellaneous	Ref Map Zillebeke Sheets 28 N W 4 & NE 3 Parts Of		
War Diary Miscellaneous	Hill 60 Sector Refce Zillebeke 28 NW 4 NE 3	03/09/1914	04/09/1914
War Diary Miscellaneous	Hill 60 Sector	04/09/1914	05/09/1914
War Diary Miscellaneous	Hill 60 Sector Ref Zillebeke 28 N.W. 4 & N.E. 3	06/04/1919	06/04/1919
War Diary Miscellaneous	Hill 60 Sector	07/09/1914	08/09/1914
War Diary Miscellaneous	Hill 60 Sector	08/09/1914	09/09/1914
War Diary Miscellaneous	Hill 60 Sector	10/09/1914	10/09/1914
War Diary Miscellaneous	Hill 60 Sector	11/09/1914	11/09/1914
War Diary Miscellaneous	Hill 60 Sector	13/09/1914	14/09/1914
War Diary Miscellaneous	Hill 60 Sector	15/09/1914	15/09/1914
Miscellaneous Miscellaneous	Hill Top Sector	16/09/1914	18/09/1914
War Diary	Hill 60 Sector	18/09/1914	20/09/1914

Miscellaneous War Diary	Hill 60 Sector	20/09/1914	22/09/1914
Miscellaneous War Diary	Hill 60 Sector	23/09/1914	25/09/1914
Miscellaneous War Diary	Hill 60 Sector	26/09/1914	26/09/1914
Miscellaneous War Diary	Hill 60 Sector	26/09/1914	28/09/1914
Miscellaneous War Diary	Berthen Area	29/09/1914	30/09/1914
Miscellaneous Miscellaneous	Appendix No 1		
Miscellaneous Miscellaneous	Appendix No 2		
Miscellaneous Miscellaneous	Appendix No 3 Instructions For Barrage fire	18/09/1917	18/09/1917
Miscellaneous Miscellaneous	Appendix 4		
Miscellaneous Miscellaneous	Appendix No 5 Operation Orders	25/09/1917	25/09/1917
Miscellaneous Miscellaneous	Appendix No 6	26/09/1917	26/09/1917
Miscellaneous Miscellaneous	39th Division	12/11/1917	12/11/1917
Miscellaneous Heading	War Diary From 1st October 1917-31st October 1917 Vol 4		
Miscellaneous War Diary	Berthen Area	01/10/1917	04/10/1917
Miscellaneous War Diary	Berthen Area	05/10/1917	07/10/1917
Miscellaneous War Diary	Berthen Area	07/10/1917	10/10/1917
Miscellaneous War Diary	Berthen Area	11/10/1917	13/10/1917
Miscellaneous War Diary	Berthen Area	14/10/1917	15/10/1917
Miscellaneous War Diary	Berthen Area	15/10/1917	15/10/1917
Miscellaneous War Diary	Berthen Area	15/10/1917	15/10/1917
War Diary	Tower Hamlets Sector	16/10/1917	16/10/1917
Miscellaneous War Diary	Tower Hamlets Sector	17/10/1917	18/10/1917
Miscellaneous War Diary	Tower Hamlets Sector	19/10/1917	19/10/1917
Miscellaneous War Diary	Tower Hamlets Sector	20/10/1917	22/10/1917
Miscellaneous War Diary	Tower Hamlet Sector	23/10/1917	23/10/1917
Miscellaneous War Diary	Tower Hamlets Sector	24/10/1917	24/10/1917
Miscellaneous War Diary	Carnarvon Camp (M 10 B 7.3)	25/10/1917	26/10/1917
Miscellaneous War Diary	Carnarvon Camp	27/10/1917	28/10/1917

War Diary	Tower Hamlets Sector	29/10/1917	29/10/1917
Miscellaneous			
War Diary	Tower Hamlets Sector	29/10/1917	29/10/1917
Miscellaneous			
Miscellaneous	Tower Hamlets Sector	29/10/1917	30/10/1917
Miscellaneous			
War Diary	Tower Hamlets Sector	30/10/1917	31/10/1917
Miscellaneous			
Miscellaneous	Appendix No 1	14/10/1917	14/10/1917
Miscellaneous	Operation Order By Capt J A Rayds Comdg 228 M.G. Coy. Appendix No. 2	23/10/1917	23/10/1917
Miscellaneous			
Miscellaneous	Operations Orders By Capt J.A. Rayds, Comdg. 228 M.G. Coy. Appendix No. 3	28/10/1917	28/10/1917
Miscellaneous	30 Division		
Miscellaneous			
Heading	War Diary For 1st November 1917-30th November 1917 Volume 5		
Miscellaneous			
War Diary	Tower Hamlets Sector Refce Map Zillebeke 1/10,000 28 N.W.4 N.E. 3	01/11/1917	01/11/1917
Miscellaneous			
War Diary	Tower Hamlets Sector Maps Zillebeke Shrewsbury Forest 1/10,000	02/11/1917	03/11/1917
Miscellaneous			
War Diary	Tower Hamlets Sector	04/11/1917	04/11/1917
Miscellaneous			
War Diary	Tower Hamlet Sector	05/11/1917	05/11/1917
Miscellaneous			
War Diary	Tower Hamlets Sector	06/11/1917	06/11/1917
Miscellaneous			
War Diary	Tower Hamlets Sector	06/11/1917	07/11/1917
Miscellaneous			
Miscellaneous	Tower Hamlets Sector	08/11/1917	09/11/1917
Miscellaneous			
War Diary	Tower Hamlet Sector	09/11/1917	10/11/1917
Miscellaneous			
War Diary	Menin Road Sector Ref Map Gheluvelt 1/10,000 Sheet 28 NE 3	11/11/1917	12/11/1917
Miscellaneous			
War Diary	Menin Road Sector	12/11/1917	14/11/1917
Miscellaneous			
War Diary	Menin Road Sector	14/11/1917	15/11/1917
Miscellaneous			
War Diary	Menin Road Sector	16/11/1917	16/11/1917
Miscellaneous			
War Diary	Menin Road Sector	17/11/1917	17/11/1917
Miscellaneous			
War Diary	Menin Rd Sector	19/11/1917	20/11/1917
Miscellaneous			
War Diary	Menin Road Sector	21/11/1917	21/11/1917
Miscellaneous			
War Diary	Menin Road Sector	22/11/1917	23/11/1917
Miscellaneous			
War Diary	Menin Road Sector	23/11/1917	24/11/1917
Miscellaneous			

War Diary	Menin Road Sector	25/11/1917	26/11/1917
Miscellaneous			
War Diary	Menin Road Sector To Ridge Wood	26/11/1917	26/11/1917
War Diary	Caestre Ref Map Belgium Pt Of France Sheet 27 1/40,000	27/11/1917	27/11/1917
Miscellaneous			
War Diary	Caestre Ref Map Belgium Pt Of France Sheet No 27 1/40000	27/11/1917	30/11/1917
Miscellaneous			
Miscellaneous	Operation Orders by Lieut R.W. Tyffe Acting O.C. 228 M.G. Coy. Appendix I	10/11/1917	10/11/1917
Miscellaneous			
Miscellaneous	Operation Orders By Lieut B.W. Tyffe Acting O.C. 228 M.G. Coy. Appendix II	23/11/1917	23/11/1917
Miscellaneous			
Miscellaneous	Appendix III	26/11/1917	26/11/1917
Miscellaneous			
Heading	War Diary December 1917 228 Coy Machine Gun Corps Vol 6		
Miscellaneous			
War Diary	Between Caestre & St. Sylvestre Cappel	01/12/1917	01/12/1917
War Diary	Refce Map Hazebrouck 5a 1/100,000	02/12/1917	04/12/1917
Miscellaneous			
War Diary		05/12/1917	06/12/1917
Miscellaneous			
War Diary		07/12/1917	07/12/1917
Miscellaneous			
War Diary	Val De Lumbres Refce Map Hazebrouck 5a 1/100,000	08/12/1917	28/12/1917
Miscellaneous			
War Diary	Refce Map Hazebrouck 5A 1/100,000 Sheet 28		
Miscellaneous			
War Diary		28/12/1917	29/12/1917
Miscellaneous			
War Diary		29/12/1917	31/12/1917
Miscellaneous			
War Diary		31/12/1917	31/12/1917
Miscellaneous			
Miscellaneous	39th Division		
Miscellaneous			
War Diary	St Julien Sector Ref Map Poelcappelle Spriet 1/10,000	01/01/1918	01/01/1918
Miscellaneous			
War Diary	St Julien Sector	02/01/1918	03/01/1918
Miscellaneous			
War Diary	St. Julien Sector	02/01/1918	04/01/1918
Miscellaneous			
War Diary	St. Julien Sector	04/01/1918	06/01/1918
Miscellaneous			
War Diary	St. Julien Sector	06/01/1918	07/01/1918
Miscellaneous			
War Diary	St. Julien Sector	07/01/1918	07/01/1918
Miscellaneous			
War Diary	St. Julien Sector	08/01/1918	08/01/1918
Miscellaneous			
War Diary	St. Julien Sector	09/01/1918	11/01/1918
Miscellaneous			
War Diary	St Julien Sector	11/01/1918	11/01/1918

Miscellaneous War Diary	St. Julien Sector	12/01/1918	13/01/1918
Miscellaneous War Diary	St Julien Sector	13/01/1918	15/01/1918
Miscellaneous War Diary	St. Julien Sector	15/01/1918	16/01/1918
Miscellaneous War Diary	St Julien Sector	16/01/1918	17/01/1918
Miscellaneous War Diary	St. Julien Sector	17/01/1918	18/01/1918
Miscellaneous War Diary	St. Julien Sector	19/01/1918	20/01/1918
Miscellaneous War Diary	St. Julien Sector	20/01/1918	21/01/1918
War Diary	Tunnellers Camp	22/01/1918	24/01/1918
Miscellaneous War Diary	Tunnellers Camp	25/01/1918	25/01/1918
War Diary	Morcourt	26/01/1918	28/01/1918
Miscellaneous War Diary	Morcourt	28/01/1918	29/01/1918
War Diary	Haut Allaines	30/01/1918	31/01/1918
Miscellaneous War Diary	Gouzeaucort Sector	01/02/1918	01/02/1918
Miscellaneous War Diary	Gouzeacourt Sector	01/02/1918	02/02/1918
Miscellaneous War Diary	Gouzeaucourt Sector	02/02/1918	03/02/1918
Miscellaneous War Diary	Gouzeaucourt Sector	04/02/1918	05/02/1918
Miscellaneous War Diary	Gouzeaucourt Sector	06/02/1918	07/02/1918
Miscellaneous War Diary	Gouzeaucourt Sector	08/02/1918	09/02/1918
Miscellaneous War Diary	Gouzeaucourt Sector	09/02/1918	10/02/1918
Miscellaneous War Diary	Gouzeaucourt Sector	11/02/1918	12/02/1918
Miscellaneous War Diary	Gouzeacourt Sector	12/02/1918	13/02/1918
Miscellaneous War Diary	Gouzeacourt Sector	14/02/1918	15/02/1918
Miscellaneous War Diary	Gouzeacourt Sector	15/02/1918	16/02/1918
Miscellaneous War Diary	Gouzeacourt Sector	16/02/1918	17/02/1918
Miscellaneous War Diary	Gouzeacourt Sector	17/02/1918	18/02/1918
Miscellaneous War Diary	Gouzeacourt Sector	16/02/1918	19/02/1918
Miscellaneous War Diary	Gouzeacourt Sector	20/02/1918	20/02/1918
Miscellaneous War Diary	Gouzeacourt Sector	21/02/1918	22/02/1918
Miscellaneous War Diary	Gouzeacourt Sector	22/02/1918	24/02/1918
Miscellaneous			

War Diary Miscellaneous	Gouzeacourt Sector	24/02/1918	25/02/1918
War Diary Miscellaneous	Gouzeacourt Sector	26/02/1918	27/02/1918
War Diary Miscellaneous	Gouzeacourt Sector	28/02/1918	28/02/1918

W095/25775

39TH DIVISION

228TH MACHINE GUN COY.

JLY 1917-~~MAR 1919~~.

Dec 1917

(Includes Jan + Feb 1918)

Confidential

War Diary

of

from 12th July 1917. to 31st July 1917.

Volume. 1.

Jly '17
79

Army Form C. 2118.

WAR DIARY
or
INTELLIGENCE SUMMARY.
(Erase heading not required.)

Instructions regarding War Diaries and Intelligence Summaries are contained in F. S. Regs., Part II. and the Staff Manual respectively. Title pages will be prepared in manuscript.

Place	Date	Hour	Summary of Events and Information	Remarks and references to Appendices
Le Havre	1917 12/4	am 10.30 p.m 3.30 5.30	Disembarked. Moved off to Rest Camp. Arrived at No 1 Camp. Accomodation 16 tents for ORs	Strength 10 officers 178 O. Ranks
	13/4	11 am	Inspection of Camp & Lines by Camp Commandant - Col Parker. Special Inspection under Camp arrangements Gas Helmets & Small Box Respirators. Report submitted to HQ (No1 Camp) re defaulters etc. Gas cleaning parade Casualties 1 OR admitted to Hospital Sick	
	14/4		Heavy thunder - Rovers up to 10.30 am Daily Inspection of lines by Camp Commandant Physical Training, Gas cleaning parades during morning Coy marched down to Beach for bathing 5 new mules arrived from Remounts Depot to replace those evacuated at Skampton	
	15/4	1.45 pm	Horse Inspection & another bathing parade 1 Riding Horse & 1 Mule Cart replaced	
	16/4		2nd Lieut R.J. Aldridge admitted to Hospital with Pleurisy	Evacuated S.S. 9-4938

Army Form C. 2118.

WAR DIARY
or
INTELLIGENCE SUMMARY.
(Erase heading not required.)

Instructions regarding War Diaries and Intelligence Summaries are contained in F. S. Regs., Part II. and the Staff Manual respectively. Title pages will be prepared in manuscript.

Place	Date	Hour	Summary of Events and Information	Remarks and references to Appendices
Le Havre	14/4	9am	Coy for Route march kit 12.30pm.	
		8.30pm	Received orders to move at 6.30am tomorrow	
	15/4	11am	Reveille. Breakfast 5am. Moved off at 6.30am followed by 225 MG Coy. Two complete companies with Transport vehicles + animals on one train	
		8am	Entrained 26 men per truck	
		8.25pm	Arrived Abbeville. about 30 minutes rest.	
	19/4	6am	Arrived POPERINGHE. Met up a guide from 39th Division	Strengths 8 officers 90 14 yrs
		7.15am	Marched off to 39th Division HQ shop Ref G.6.B.2.8 BELGIUM 28 N.W. 1/20,000	
		9.30am	Arrived C Camp in wood No accommodation but informed Tents would be moved later. Transport to G.5.A.5.u.	
		8pm	Took over ex watchup tents. Ample accommodation A.30.D.14 } BELGIUM 28 N.W.	

Army Form C. 2118.

WAR DIARY
or
INTELLIGENCE SUMMARY.
(Erase heading not required.)

Instructions regarding War Diaries and Intelligence Summaries are contained in F.S. Regs., Part II. and the Staff Manual respectively. Title pages will be prepared in manuscript.

Place	Date	Hour	Summary of Events and Information	Remarks and references to Appendices
POPERINGHE AREA	20/7		O.C. up to Line (HILLTOP SECTOR) with D.M.G.O. 10 am – 11.30 am	
	21/7		O.C. with 1st & 2nd officers of No 1 Section rode up to CANAL BANK to arrange re relief of guns. Reported to 33rd Bde H.Q. 11 am. 4 guns to relieve 4 guns of No 116 M.G. Coy. Remaining 12 guns to be in reserve in CANAL BANK.	Relief
		6.30 pm	Coy moved off from 'C' Camp. No 1 Section leading.	
		11 pm	Reported "Relief Complete". Gun position at { LA BRIQUE / WILSON FARM N / — / ZOUAVE VILLA } Long Range "Harassing Fire" carried out at irregular intervals from 11.30 to 3 am. Systematic searching & traversing of selected areas before enemy lines. No. of rounds fired 6,000 approx. Targets in area C1 y a. b & c etc. Ref St Julien 28 NW2. 1/10,000. CANAL BANK bombarded with Gas Shells 12.30 – 2am. Casualties 3 men wounded at REIGERSBURG CHATEAU on way up to line	Night firing
	22/7		Working party consisting of 16 men & 2 NCOs supposed to assist in construction of MG emplacements for guns during barrage fire on 'Z' day. Carrying party supplied for SAA in order to MG camp.	Work

Army Form C. 2118.

WAR DIARY
or
INTELLIGENCE SUMMARY.
(Erase heading not required.)

Instructions regarding War Diaries and Intelligence Summaries are contained in F. S. Regs., Part II. and the Staff Manual respectively. Title pages will be prepared in manuscript.

Place	Date	Hour	Summary of Events and Information	Remarks and references to Appendices
HILL TOP SECTOR	1914 28/4	9.30pm	Harassing fire by 8 guns – 100.192 sections Targets mostly about 1,000 behind enemy front line Object to harass the open between hand communication trenches into which our Artillery were dealing & so cater parties coming from trenches Map reference of targets ST JULIEN 28 NW2 1/10,000 No 1 Sect { C14 c 85.41 to C 6.80 ; C14 d 26.90 to 6.50.10 ; C14 b 05.30 to a 55.45 ; C14 a 20.50 to b 85.80 } No 2 Sect { C14 a 45.45 to 116.05.85 ; C14 b 62.90 to b 85.9a ; C10 d 45.00 to d 35.25 ; C19 a 98.30 to a 60.90 } Casualties 1 man admitted to 34P act Large number of flares fired but over between 12 midnight and 3am in vicinity of gun positions and along CANAL BANK During day men of 3 & 4 Sections employed carrying ammunition and constructing MG emplacements	Totalrs fired. 21,500 Time 9.30 to 3am.
	28/4	9.30pm	Harassing fire carried out by 8 guns of Nos 1 & 2 Sections Same targets as previous night 9.30pm to 3am. Gas shells on CANAL BANK again between 12.9.2.30am Vicinity of IRISH FARM shelled fairly heavily about 2am Casualties: 1 killed CANAL BANK 1 wounded MG sick 1 admitted 34P sect	Total Rds 20,800
	29/4		Working parties supplied by No 3 & 4 Sections during day as before	Sec. of Corps. 0.9 4 79.1

WAR DIARY or INTELLIGENCE SUMMARY

Army Form C. 2118.

Place	Date	Hour	Summary of Events and Information	Remarks and references to Appendices
HILL TOP SECTOR. Refce. map St. JULIEN 28 N.W.2 1/10,000	24/4		Nos 3 & 4 Sections detailed to give supporting fire in connection with a raid to be carried out on CANADIAN TRENCH at 4:30 a.m. by a Coy of 9th S.Rwoods. Guns and ammunition etc carried up during day to get into position before dusk. Guns layed for harassing fire during night & in addition to raid at dawn. No 1 Section keyed to carry ammunition for Rege guns. No 2 Section supplied working party. Zones 2-10 p.m.	
		9:30 p.m.	Harassing {C16 d 56.42 to 56.00 2,450 Rounds C16 a 90.04 . 6.25.94 3,000 Fire {C17 c 84.00 . 04.38 2,500 C17 d 04.38 . 04.60 3,000 Targets 11,250	Rounds 22,500
		2:30 a.m.		
		4:30 a.m. – 5 a.m.	Angles during raid {C16 d 44.42 to 56.53 C16 a 49.40 . 55.28 C15 b 63.15 . 42.20 C15 b 94.28 . 94.05 C16 c 80.50 . d 20.30	C 17C 35.00 to 40.45 5,500 C 16 b 60.50 . 23.00 3,000 C 16 a 98.80 . 15.90 2,750 11,250 Total Rounds fired 12,900 Casualties (Killed) (Gas) 6 ORs
	25/4		Enemy Gas Shells distributed at regular intervals between 12:30 + 3:30 am in areas C29a, C29b, C20, C82, WILSON FARM & CANAL BANK Weather Very misty about 4 am. Heavy rain later up to 11am.	Strength of Coy 4+65 ORs

Army Form C. 2118.

WAR DIARY
or
INTELLIGENCE SUMMARY.
(Erase heading not required.)

Instructions regarding War Diaries and Intelligence Summaries are contained in F.S. Regs., Part II. and the Staff Manual respectively. Title pages will be prepared in manuscript.

Place	Date	Hour	Summary of Events and Information	Remarks and references to Appendices
HILL TOP SECTOR Ref map ST JULIEN 28 NW 2 1/10,000	25/4		Working Party of 2 NCOs & 18 men employed on M.G. Emplacements for barrage fire on Z day 2 pm to 11 pm. Relieved 5 guns of 232 M.G. Coy (51st Div) w/the plan 2 guns of No 1 Sect at HILLTOP FARM 1 " " No 3 " BELLE ALLIANCE 1 " " " BILGE TRENCH 1 " " " IRISH FARM <u>Note</u> 4 guns still remaining in daylight defensive positions as taken over on 21/4/17 namely 1 at LA BRIQUE, 2 at WILSON FARM, 1 at ZOUAVE VILLA & 1 at CANAL BANK. Guns doing Harassing fire by night with 4 more teams guns from CANAL BANK.	
	26/4	9.30 pm to 3 am	Harassing Fire Targets C. 17 C. 84 . L 68 3,000 Rds C.14a.4545 K.11c.0505 2,500 Rds C. 14d. 24.70 . 30.98 2250 C.10d.45.00 3525 2450 C. 14c. 5530 . 32.65 2450 C.16a.98.80 5090 3000 8,000 16,250 8,250 Casualties 4 ORs wounded 4 OR admitted SAP each	Rds 16,250

Army Form C. 2118.

WAR DIARY
or
INTELLIGENCE SUMMARY

(Erase heading not required.)

Instructions regarding War Diaries and Intelligence Summaries are contained in F.S. Regs., Part II. and the Staff Manual respectively. Title pages will be prepared in manuscript.

Place	Date	Hour	Summary of Events and Information	Remarks and references to Appendices
HILLTOP SECTOR Ref Map ST JULIEN	13/4/.		No 2 Section relieved No 1 Section at the 4 daylight positions	
			Carrying parties supplied for taking ammunition to M.G. dumps also for work on M.G. emplacements all for 7 days	
23 N.W.2 I/10,000			Harrassing fire Targets	
			C 16 b 50.50 to 30.40 4000 Rds	
			C 16a 95.50. 15.90 3600 -	P.16 15/50
			Only 4 guns available owing C 17c 55.20 . 32.65 4000	
			to working parties etc. C 17c 85.41 80.50 4250	
			Total 15,750 Rds	
	24/4		Working parties as before on M.G. emplacements	
			Rumours received that enemy had retired to the Black line	
			33rd Bde. Propose to push forward 6th June & 4th K.S. Staffs – I report proves true, to	
			hold enemy line & send out patrols forward to locate enemy.	
			225 M.G. Coy. to hold guns in readiness to go forward & Rep. to hold line if necessary	0.36. 9.4.5.cr
			Patrols sent out later found line to be still occupied & met with determined resistance	9.4.5.cr
			Casualties 1 O.R. Killed. 1 O.R. wounded.	

Army Form C. 2118.

WAR DIARY
or
INTELLIGENCE SUMMARY.
(Erase heading not required.)

Place	Date	Hour	Summary of Events and Information	Remarks and references to Appendices
HILL TOP SECTOR Ref Map ST JULIEN 28NW2 1/10,000	28/9		Owing to "Warning Order" received for guns to prepare to move forward yesterday evening. It was impossible to carry out the normal "Harassing fire" from 9.30 to 3am	
		5.15am	A Chinese Raid arranged on our front for 5.15am. 4 guns of No 2 Sect. supplied intense fire from 5.15 to 5.30am	

			Targets { C16b 20+0 2,590 Rounds
			        { C16c 6060 1,500
			        { C16c 9090 1,860
			        { C16a 8060 2,090
			 Total 7,850 Rounds
				Rounds 7,850

			33rd Bde H.Q. on CANAL BANK relieved by 116th Bde 39th Div Working Party of 14 men + 2 NCOs on M.G. emplacements front to fire	

		9.30am to 3am	Targets { C16a 9510 to 6.3510 4,000 C16a 6070 to 6060 3,000
			        { C16b 3590 6.6545 4,000 C Nd 3565 9.9010 4,000
			        { C16d 6060 6.6010 3,500 C. 7a 9030 5050 3,450
			 Harassing fire 11,500 10,450
				Rds. 22,250

		10am to 3am	Heavy Bombardment of CANAL BANK and Gun Screens	

Army Form C. 2118.

WAR DIARY
or
INTELLIGENCE SUMMARY.
(Erase heading not required.)

Instructions regarding War Diaries and Intelligence Summaries are contained in F. S. Regs., Part II. and the Staff Manual respectively. Title pages will be prepared in manuscript.

Place	Date	Hour	Summary of Events and Information	Remarks and references to Appendices

HILL TOP SECTOR Ref Map ST. JULIEN 28 N.W.2 France	29/4		Heavy rain started 9am. No 1 Section relieved No.4. No 2 Sect. relieved No 3 in consideration of the fact that No 3 & No 4 Scots may be detailed to go forward on Z day. Instruction from 118th Bde HQ. to allot special S.O.S. targets to guns in case of enemy raid on our line C.15c 80.35 to C21 6.30 60 in front of HORNBY TRENCH.
			
			 TARGETS:
			 Maximum { C.16a 50.10 to 90.40 2,500 Rds
			 { C.16c 80.00 - 20.29 2,500
			 Blue { C.16c 05.32 22.40 2,000
			 { C.15d 80.80 CANADIAN LANE 2,250
			                                    ————
			                                     9,250
			
			 CANADIAN RESERVE 2,000 Rds
			 C 16a.95.10 to B 35.40 }
			 C 16c.35.40 to 65.45 } 3,450
			                          ————
			                           5,450
			
			 Note Small expenditure of ammunition owing to scarce requiring in of S.O.S signal
			
			 Casualties - 1 Rule wounded
				Rds 15,870
				
				 Strength of day
				 9 nsors
				
				 [signature]

Army Form C. 2118.

WAR DIARY
or
INTELLIGENCE SUMMARY.
(Erase heading not required.)

Place	Date	Hour	Summary of Events and Information	Remarks and references to Appendices
HILL TOP SECTOR Ref. Map. St. Julien 28 N.W.2. 1/10,000	30th		8 guns to fire at the rate of 30 rounds per minute from Zero - Zero + 7ero to cover the noise made by Tanks moving to the Starting Point near our front line. Each gun to fire a burst in turn so as to produce a continuous crack. Target to be as normally engaged in Harassing Fire. 6 guns to fire one line in the following positions:- 1) HILLTOP N. (2) HILLTOP S. (3) LA BELLE ALLIANCE. (4) IRISHFARM. (5) BILGE TRENCH (6) THREADNEEDLE ST. The 8 guns employed in Harassing fire to be prepared to advance 4 ZERO Hour fixed for 3.50 a.m	
	31st	1.50 am to 3.50 am	TARGETS C.14.d. 5530 6.3265 2000 C.16.6. 3565 6.7545 2,800. C.14.c. 8541 · 6.080 3000 C.16.0. 5010 · 7040 · 1,750 C.14.2. 2940 · 30.98 2,300 C.16.0. 8000 · 30.27 1,500 C.16.a. 9510 · 6.3060 2,600 C.16.0. 0532 · 2240 2,050 9,350 7,250	Rds. 16,850

Army Form C. 2118.

WAR DIARY
or
INTELLIGENCE SUMMARY.
(Erase heading not required.)

Place	Date	Hour	Summary of Events and Information	Remarks and references to Appendices
HILL TOP. Sector Ref. Map St Julien 28 N W 2. 1/10,000	21st	4pm	Received orders to relieve 9 guns of 145 hr.S.Coy. in vicinity of MOUSE TRAP FARM. O.C. + a Section officer up to reconnoitre positions 8pm. Raining steadily all evening. Officers 9/c of 145 Co guns decided relief could be completed not at dawn. Guns arrived at position + am Aug 21st	

228 M.G. Coy
Army Form C. 2118.

WAR DIARY
or
INTELLIGENCE SUMMARY
(Erase heading not required.)

Vol 2

Place	Date	Hour	Summary of Events and Information	Remarks and references to Appendices
N. of YPRES HILL TOP SECTOR	1917 Aug 1st	11 am	9 Guns relieved 9 Guns of 145 by 9 Corp in old German 1st Support line near MOUSETRAP FARM. Guns to be tactically under the orders of 116th Inf. Bde whose H.Q.rs are established	
Map Ref Sh. St Julien 28 NW2 1/10000			about 300x distant in old German front line. Normally the guns are for defensive purposes & to form a "Protective Barrage" along the line C.b.c.14 to C.12.b.5.65 (approx 1000x) about 300x beyond the far bank of the STEENBECK. Fire to be opened in case of S.O.S signal from our own front line. Weather Rain had been falling heavily throughout the night & continued most of the day. The Road via HILLTOP & running across late "NO MANS LAND" towards MOUSETRAP FARM is in a terrible state owing to the continual traffic of heavy guns, ammunition, supplies, etc. Throughout July 31st & Aug 1st Trenches, whole were practically non-existent also in a terrible state of mud & debris. Gun positions selected in the open making use of Shell holes half full of water. Approx positions C.16.d.50.75	Strength O.R's 9.155 "Dorset"/Major 4 + 45

Army Form C. 2118.

WAR DIARY
or
INTELLIGENCE SUMMARY.
(Erase heading not required.)

Place	Date	Hour	Summary of Events and Information	Remarks and references to Appendices
N. of YPRES HILL TOP SECTOR map Ref. St JULIEN 28NW2 1/10,000	Aug 1st		Gun positions manned throughout day in pouring rain. Shelling intermittent all day - apparently with no definite target but distributed over open ground along enemy old front line system. A great deal of movement over by own troops but observation very poor owing to rain & dull light - No Aircraft up at all.	
	2d		The same adverse conditions still exist - rain continues & it is almost impossible to get about. The conditions have certainly delayed our progress. A Coy. buried with 2 mules was sent up to carry material for construction of canal & shelters etc. to gun positions, but only managed to get half way. One mule was badly stuck in the mud & could not be extricated from the hole, eventually died of exhaustion.	
		P.M. 9.40	S.O.S. signal observed on our front - all fire my guns opened fire as far as possible arranged & continued till 9.55 p.m. Total rounds fired 2,150	R/o 2,150
			Casualties 1 Sergt. 1 Cpl. & 1 Pte wounded at gun positions	Strength 9 4/55

Army Form C. 2118.

WAR DIARY
or
INTELLIGENCE SUMMARY.
(Erase heading not required.)

Place	Date	Hour	Summary of Events and Information	Remarks and references to Appendices
N. of YPRES HILL TOP SECTOR Map Ref ST JULIEN 28NW2 1/10000	Aug 2nd	11am	6 Guns withdrawn from original ParkoB lines making 8 guns in reserve at CANAL BANK	
		4:30 pm	Nos 1 & 2 Sections relieved Nos 3 & 4 Sections at MOUSE TRAP FARM. Guns & ammunition were taken over as they stood to avoid unnecessary carrying through the mud. A Buying Shed was prepared at CANAL BANK & a change of lines for No. 3 & 4 Sections on their return.	
			Intermittent shelling continued day and night in vicinity of gun positions particularly active between 2 & 4 am.	
	3rd		Weather conditions still very bad. Raining steadily all day. Shelling as usual but more intense at night. Enemy artillery appeared to be traversing CALF RESERVE 6-10 pm.	
			S.O.S. Signal went up again at 9.40 pm on our front. 8 Guns fired on S.O.S. Barrage line 9.40 - 9.55 pm. Total Rounds fired 1,500	Rds 1,500
			5 guns at C.16 d.50.45 (approx) Range 2250ˣ to 2350ˣ Clearances 2 E 5° 18', to 6° 8', Target Mag Bearing 49° to 59°0 86 to 112ˣ	
			3 guns at C.16d.25.95 (approx) Range 2,400ˣ - 2 E 9.0' Clearances Mag Bearing 58° to 63° 184ˣ	
			Note: Own troops assumed at 1900ˣ & 2050ˣ from guns respectively for calculating clearance	Strength 9 & 155 OR Horses Mules 7 & 441

Army Form C. 2118.

WAR DIARY
or
INTELLIGENCE SUMMARY.
(Erase heading not required.)

Instructions regarding War Diaries and Intelligence Summaries are contained in F. S. Regs., Part II. and the Staff Manual respectively. Title pages will be prepared in manuscript.

Place	Date	Hour	Summary of Events and Information	Remarks and references to Appendices
N.of YPRES	Aug 1st	6 am	Nos 3+4 Sections relieved Nos 1+2 Sections – Owing to the trying conditions in the open,	
HILL TOP SECTOR map Ref.			Gun teams are being relieved once every 36 hrs. Ref. any guns still in Divisional Reserve.	
			One gun + tripod with 6 belt boxes blown up + absolutely demolished just before gun teams were relieved. No casualties.	
St JULIEN				
28 NW 2 1/10,000			Weather. Rain lifting almost for first time since the night of July 31st. Bright intervals + Aircraft at work again	
	August 2nd		A fine day for a change	
			Nos 1+2 Sections cleaned guns + packed limbers at CANAL BANK in preparation	
			for the Divisional move + at 2.30 p.m. moved to bivouacs at REIGERSBURG CHATEAU	
			about ½ a mile back	
			Relief 8 guns at MOUSETRAP FARM relieved by 6 guns of 143/144 Inf. Coy 48th Div.	
			Guides met incoming teams at ESSEX FARM 4 p.m.	
			Relief complete about 7 p.m.	

Army Form C. 2118.

WAR DIARY
or
INTELLIGENCE SUMMARY.
(Erase heading not required.)

Instructions regarding War Diaries and Intelligence Summaries are contained in F. S. Regs., Part II. and the Staff Manual respectively. Title pages will be prepared in manuscript.

Place	Date	Hour	Summary of Events and Information	Remarks and references to Appendices
CANAL BANK HILL-TOP SECTOR	6th Aug		Nos 3 & 4 Sections cleaning guns & packing limbers preparatory to Divisional move tomorrow	
	7th		Orders to march with 118th Bde	
		9.30 am	Moved off from CANAL BANK to VLAMERTINGHE	
		11.40 am	Entrained	
		12.15 pm	Arrived CAESTRE	
		1.40 pm	Motor lorries conveyed us to THIESHOUK	
			March to PIEBROUCK arriving about 6.30 pm	
			Very good billets at farm house exactly suitable for the accommodation of Co.	
			Complete No 9 Coy with Transport	
PIEBROUCK	8th		OC rode to 118th Bde Hd at THIESHOUK & on to CAESTRE also on to FLETRE & on to BAILLEUL endeavouring to find a Field Cashier. Men have had no pay since entering 11th July.	
			Heavy rain in evening	
				Strength Offrs 5 ORs Horses/Mules 7 + 46

A6945   Wt. W14422/M1160   350,000   12/16   D. D. & L.   Forms/C./2118/14

Army Form C. 2118.

WAR DIARY
INTELLIGENCE SUMMARY.
(Erase heading not required.)

Place	Date	Hour	Summary of Events and Information	Remarks and references to Appendices
PIEBROUCK	Aug 9th		Opened Imprest Account Field Cashier BAILLEUL 2nd Anzac Corps	
hop Refce			Drew £co 2000	
R 24 a 39			Paid company 4 km	
Belgium &			Parades as yesterday - Physical training - Gun Cleaning - Immediate Action	
France			(9.30 - 12.30 & 2 - 3.30 Pm)	
Sheet 27				
1/40,000	10th		Parades as usual 9.30 - 12.30 & 2 - 3.30. Limbers washed & wheels filled with grease. 12 draft	new names
	11th		Parades as usual.	
			O.C. to Due HQ at METEREN to meet D.M.G.O. with reference to relief	
			of guns in the line (HOLLEBEKE)	
	12th		O.C. 2nd I/C + one Sect Officer up to line to reconnoitre pst PIEBROUCK 7.30 am	
			Met G.O. H/e Div at 124th Bdgr. HQ	
			Rode about 9 miles & walked 2½ miles to see D.M.G.O with O.C. 238 M.G.C. on line. Back at	
			in the BLUFF von to arrange relief	
		4 P.M.		

WAR DIARY or INTELLIGENCE SUMMARY

Army Form C. 2118.

Place	Date	Hour	Summary of Events and Information	Remarks and references to Appendices
	12th		Bde Siv Order No 139 (Re 39th Div (less Artillery) will relieve the 41st Division (less Artillery) in the HOLLEBEKE-KLEIN ZILLEBEKE Sector	
			116th Infy Bde. relieves 122nd Bde on night 13/14th	
			Holding front from TORRET FARM to YPRES - COMINES CANAL	
			117th Infy Bde. relieves 124th Bde on night of 14/15th holding front from YPRES-COMINES CANAL to ZWARTELEN - KLEINZILLEBEKE Rd.	
			118th Infy Bde. in Divl Reserve in RIDGEWOOD (N5a area)	
			228 M.G. Coy (less 1 Sect) & Sects of 116 M.G.C. will relieve 236 M.G.C. in positions about IMPERIAL SWITCH on night of 14/15th. 1 Section 228 M.G.C. to be in Divl reserve in RIDGE WOOD.	
	13th		Moved from PIEBROUCK to RIDGE WOOD under orders of 117th Infy Bde.	
		4.45	Marched off to em-bussing point - LA FLETRE - METEREN RD W.12.b.8.3.	
			Arrived em-bussing point 6 am. Moved off about 7 pm.	
		9 pm	De-bussed. LA CLYTE - DICKEBUSH RD. AT HALLEBAST CORNER	
			Marched to RIDGE WOOD. Bivouacked about N.5.c.19.97. FRANCE 28 SW 1/20,000	Trench Maps
			Coy Transport-lines at M.10.c.1.2	Q.4/6/4/80

WAR DIARY
or
INTELLIGENCE SUMMARY.
(Erase heading not required.)

Army Form C. 2118.

Place	Date	Hour	Summary of Events and Information	Remarks and references to Appendices
RIDGE	Aug 14th	3am	All guns & tripods packed on one limber & sent up to the line with a No 1 to each gun. Guides from 238 M.G Coy to meet limbers at the BRICK STACK near SPOIL BANK (~T330) at 4 a.m.	
WOOD			Conduct the party along track to gun positions & exchange guns & tripods at the emplacements	
N.5c.10.94			According to advice given there was considered the greatest hour of the day to effect the	
France 28SW			exchange. There was however heavy hostile shelling around the BRICK STACK & along	
1/20,000			the CANAL BANK at this hour & the guides did not arrive till after 6am. My party had to take the best cover possible for about 2 hours. My limber eventually getting away with the guns & tripods of 238 Coy about 8am. Fortunately no casualties—	
			Relief of Personnel. The remainder of gun numbers namely Nos 1,2,3,4,5, 6 of Nos 1,3 & 4 Sections & 1 Section of 116 Coy relieved the gun teams of 238 Coy at 2.30am making their way to gun positions in small parties.	
			The relief was carried out without much difficulty	
			OC reported to D.M.G.O. Hi⁺ Div at CANAL BANK & took over all information etc. on behalf of D.M.G.O. 39th Division	

Army Form C. 2118.

WAR DIARY
or
INTELLIGENCE SUMMARY.
(Erase heading not required.)

Place	Date	Hour	Summary of Events and Information	Remarks and references to Appendices
HOLLEBEKE	Aug		No 2 Section now in Div Reserve at RIDGE WOOD.	
SECTOR	14th		A new Coy HQ also established There in communication with 118th Bde HQ	
			Disposition on the line. The 12 guns of 228 MG Coy & 4 of 116th Coy form 2 Batteries "C" & "D" each composed of 8 guns	
			The guns to be under Battery commanders, the 2 Batteries forming a Group under a Group Commander in telephonic communication with each Battery &	
			Brigade HQ at CANAL BANK.	
			Approx positions. C Battery centre at T.34.a.9.6	
			D " T.35.b.3.8.	
			Group HQ T.34.d.5.6	
			Batteries to be prepared to create a barrage on a definite line on SOS signal back battery fires a normal SOS Target also an SOS Target on the right Auning make being laid, all calculations carefully worked out in advance. Fire can be opened on either Target at a word from Group HQ. In addition to these each battery carries out Searching fire nightly in order to facilitate control 500 squares are divided for this purpose into 4 rectangular quarters, see diagram later & calculations worked	Strength 9+461 Horse mules 7+46

WAR DIARY
or
INTELLIGENCE SUMMARY
(Erase heading not required.)

Army Form C. 2118.

Place	Date	Hour	Summary of Events and Information	Remarks and references to Appendices
HOLLEBEKE SECTOR	Aug 14th		out to the centre of the square. Runs a gun ordered to fire on 20.I would lay on the centre of square V.13. 20. 25. y5. & react N.o1 square 250x by 250x	
			Fairly quiet during day - own Artillery active	
			enemy artillery active after midnight up to 4 am.	
			Much aerial activity on both sides in evening - one of our Planes brought down.	
			Guns Done Searching fire at irregular intervals 9.30 - 3.30 am	
			Intense fire on S O S normal targets 3.30 - 3.450am	
			Targets engaged "C" Battery squares P.1, d.3, P.9, a.3 O.12.b.2 3000rds	Total 10,200 Rds
			P.1, C.4, O.12.C.2, P.1C.4	
			SOS Target P.1, C.88 to P.1.C.28 2,450 rds	
			D Battery Squads J.31.d.1,2,3,4 2,750	
			SOS Target P.1.b.48 to J.31.d.68 2,000	
	15th	5 am	Rations on way up to firing badly shelled in vicinity of VORMEZEELE Casualties Transport Sgt Killed + R.o. Roret, One driver badly wounded + 2 mules OC down from the line to report to Divisional HQ at WESTOUTRE	Strength 9 465 ORs Horses + Mules 6 + 45

WAR DIARY
or
INTELLIGENCE SUMMARY.

(Erase heading not required.)

Army Form C. 2118.

Place	Date	Hour	Summary of Events and Information	Remarks and references to Appendices
	Aug 15th		Orders from Bgd Div HQ. "In conjunction with offensive operations to be undertaken further to the North on the 16th inst. A,B,C & D M.G Batteries will open intense fire (1 belt per 2 minutes) on Barrage (S.O.S) Zones from Zero to Zero plus 30mn"	
			In accordance with this order C & D Batteries opened fire 4.45am & continued firing	
	16th	4.45	till 5.15am on S.O.S Targets P.I.C.88 & 6.28 P.1.&.48 & J.31.d.68	
		5.15am	Intense fire. Total Rounds fired by C & D Batteries 34,550.	
			The Targets engaged by A & B Batteries were	
			'A' at 0.4.a.1.5 Target 0.12.c.9.2 to 0.12.d.3.7	
			'B' at T.34.d.7.3 . 0.12.d.28 . 0.12.b.73	
			Searching fire was also carried out by C & D Batteries. Targets engaged P.1.&.3, P.1.d.1	
			P.1.d.3.4. Ammunition expended 2,500 rounds	
			Hostile Artillery shelled the vicinity of C & D Batteries intermittently throughout	Total Rds 37,050
			the night & during the Intense fire 2 guns of D Battery were buried by shells	'C' 'D'
			but not actually hit	Strength 6.45
				Horses/mules 9 & 1650 6.45

Army Form C. 2118.

WAR DIARY
or
INTELLIGENCE SUMMARY.
(Erase heading not required.)

Instructions regarding War Diaries and Intelligence Summaries are contained in F. S. Regs., Part II. and the Staff Manual respectively. Title pages will be prepared in manuscript.

Place	Date	Hour	Summary of Events and Information	Remarks and references to Appendices
HOLLEBEKE	Aug			
SECTOR	16th	11.45 am	Unusually quiet during the day. Enemy artillery fairly active during evening.	
			Whole area in vicinity of Battery M.G positions & both sides of track leading back towards	
			THE BLUFF & CANAL BANK subjected to heavy shelling.	
		12.30 am	The bombardment slackened	
	17th	3-0 am	Heavy shelling started again in same area with a few gas shells. N.E.	
		3.30	emplacement of one of my D" battery guns was knocked in & repaired during night	
			Aeroplanes both own & enemy were up between 11pm & 12.30am. A number of bombs	
			were dropped in back area behind our lines	
	Night of 16/17th		Searching Fire "C" Battery Area P.194.3 } 10pm to 4.30am 1500 rds	Total
			P.1.d.3.w.} to 12 MN 1500 rds	3,100 Rds.
			D" P.1. C.1. 2.4	
			Note. Both Batteries were ordered to cease fire temporarily during bombardment	
			Weather Still fine	
			Enemy Artillery more active during the day chiefly around the CANAL at SPOIL BANK	
	18th		RAVINE WOOD & along THE BLUFF. At night increased activity in same area, also	
			around our Batteries (M.G.) & along CATERPILLAR TRACK. Shelling was most intense	
		1.14.45am & 2 & 2.30 am		
			Aircraft again great activity on both sides during night bombing raids again took place up back areas	Hersen Bridge 6 + 45 Straight G4650R0

A6945 Wt. W11422/M1160 350,000 12/16 D. D. & L. Forms/C./2118/14.

WAR DIARY
or
INTELLIGENCE SUMMARY.
(Erase heading not required.)

Army Form C. 2118.

Place	Date	Hour	Summary of Events and Information	Remarks and references to Appendices
HOLLEBEKE SECTOR	August 14/15th night		Searching } 'C' Battery. Area Pt. a.1, O.18.d 2+3 } Time /fire } 'D' - P.1.C.1, 2+3 } 9.30pm to 4am	Rds 7,000 7,000
	15th		Enemy Artillery active throughout day mostly shelling same area as yesterday viz along CANAL also S of BATTLE WOOD From 10 to 11 pm fire was intensified in these areas & a few gas shells added.	40R ammine drops.
			Aircraft still very active. During night enemy planes were over our lines at 10pm Two bombs were dropped very near to 2 M.G. Emplacements of 'C' Battery. These were knocked in but guns not damaged & no casualties.	
			Searching fire on Areas Pt.a.3, P.1.B.1 & B.14 9.30pm to 2am. Rounds fired	2,750
	Night of 18/19		Note: Firing had to be stopped on account of enemy aircraft overhead Orders received from Division during night that there were indications of an enemy relief taking place on our front Both batteries opened fire on their Normal S.O.S. Targets 'C' Battery Target P.C.88 to P.1.B.28 - 3,500 rounds } 2 to 4.30 am 'D' - P.1.B.48 to J.31.d.68 - 4,000 - }	2,750 7,500
				Strength Horses & mules 6 + 48 9 + 169 ORs

Army Form C. 2118.

WAR DIARY
or
INTELLIGENCE SUMMARY.
(Erase heading not required.)

Place	Date	Hour	Summary of Events and Information	Remarks and references to Appendices
HOLLEBEKE Sector	Aug 19th		Enemy Artillery fairly quiet during day. Aircraft very active, one of our own M/C brought down behind our lines.	
		11.30pm	Hostile shelling commenced around the usual area – (Heavy bombardment heard N of us in direction of ST JULIEN) Shelling continued all night until 3.30am. Gas shells being much in evidence & the gas being felt right up to 3am.	
			Searching Fire by C.D. Batteries. Targets – P1k2 + C2+3, P7a1, O12 b3, 9.30.10.11am. Rounds 5,500	Rds 5,500
	20th		Quiet during day – a good deal of aerial activity especially towards evening when 2 machines apparently our own were brought down, one at 6pm in enemy lines, one at 6.30 in our own lines.	
			Enemy Artillery shelled vicinity of BATTLE WOOD heavily between 11.412km also a few gas shells K N of us.	
			Enemy Aircraft a M/c was heard flying over our own M.G. batteries at 10.30pm and at down a few shells fire near "D" Battery	
		1.0&1.5am	Green + red lights sent up in some quantity from enemys lines 11.30 – 12.30 not	
		5.15am	Suddenly a tremendous number of various coloured lights were observed all along his front but chiefly on our left. Enemy estimated to be standing to	Strongs

9 H169 OR
Horses Mules 6 M 5

Army Form C. 2118.

WAR DIARY
~~INTELLIGENCE SUMMARY.~~
(Erase heading not required.)

Place	Date	Hour	Summary of Events and Information	Remarks and references to Appendices
HOLLEBEKE Sector	Aug 20/1		"C" Battery ordered to fire 2 belts per gun on S.O.S. Barrage line.	
			Enemy Machine Guns appeared to be searching for our M.G. Batteries between 3 & 3.30 am.	
			We are seldom bothered much by their fire altho' we continually expect the Battery position to be spotted.	
			Searching fire by C & D batteries as usual 9.30 pm to 3.30am.	
			Targets engaged P.1. a.2, & r.4.) Rounds fired	
			P.1.b.1.r.C.3.) 5,450	
			Intense fire 5.15 to 5.30 am by "C" Battery	Rds
			S.O.S. Target P.1. c.88 to P.1. d.28 3,000 rds.	8,750

Strength Officers 6 O.R. Horses/Mules 6 & 45

WAR DIARY
or
INTELLIGENCE SUMMARY

Army Form C. 2118.

Place	Date	Hour	Summary of Events and Information	Remarks and references to Appendices
HOLLEBEKE SECTOR	Aug 21st		Another fairly quiet day on our front & very little activity during night. Enemy bombarded vicinity of our gun positions with H.E. 3.30–4 am & at 4.30 am appeared to traverse our front line with T.B. Shrapnel.	
			Aircraft again heard over our battery positions 10.15 pm	
			Weather fine dry spell continues	
			Searching Fire (M.G.) Targets P.1.b.1,2,3 P.1.d.1, J.31.d.2+4 Rds	Rounds 5,500
			by C+D Batteries	5,500
	22nd		Our artillery put up an intense bombardment at 9 am lasting about half an hour after remaining fairly quiet throughout night afterwards a little artillery activity on either side during day.	
			Aircraft very active throughout day. An enemy M/C observed to fall behind our lines	
		6.30 pm	Maxim again heard overhead between 9.30 & 10.30 pm.	
			Machine Gun (enemy) a gun firing to the right of our M.G. batteries about 9.30 pm.	
			Bearing (by sound) about 150° mag. takes from T.35.d.1.9.	
			Targets P.1.a.2, 3+4 Rounds } 5,600	5,600
			P.1.d.3, J.31.d.4 }	
			Searching fire by C+D batteries	
		9.30 pm to 3.30 am		Strength Officers 6 x 45 Other Ranks 9,469 ORs

Army Form C. 2118.

WAR DIARY
or
INTELLIGENCE SUMMARY.
(Erase heading not required.)

Instructions regarding War Diaries and Intelligence Summaries are contained in F. S. Regs., Part II. and the Staff Manual respectively. Title pages will be prepared in manuscript.

Place	Date	Hour	Summary of Events and Information	Remarks and references to Appendices
HOLLEBEKE SECTOR	Aug. 23rd		Slight change in weather Cloudy & gusty S.W. wind. A.m. all showers 10 a.m. No enemy observation balloons up during day except in early hours. 2 or 3 of our own went up during P.M.	
			Aircraft. Practically no machines up at all	
			Searching fire C+D batteries P,1,b,2+3 } Rounds	Rounds
			9.30 pm – 3.30 am Targets P,1,d,1+3 } 5,500	5,500
			J,31,d,3	
	24th		Still quiet during day until 8pm when N.E & Shrapnel were put over the left of gun positions THE BLUFF, DAMSTRASSE & THE WHITE CHATEAU. The latter kept open after which all was quiet.	
			Aircraft no activity owing to strong S.W wind	
			Weather Dull & Colder Inter Sectional relief carried out	
			Searching fire by C+D Targets J,31,d,1,2,3,4 } Rounds	6,000
			9.30 pm to 3.30 am P,1,b,2+3, P,1,d,1 } 6,000	
				Strength
			Normans Armies	Officers 6 + 45
				OR 9+69 880

Army Form C. 2118.

WAR DIARY
or
INTELLIGENCE SUMMARY
(Erase heading not required.)

Place	Date	Hour	Summary of Events and Information	Remarks and references to Appendices
HOLLEBEKE	Aug		Weather. Fine but cool with a fresh S.W. wind. A very dark night.	
Sector	25th		Enemy Artillery. Shelled vicinity of M.G. battery positions until H.E. 10.30 – 11.15 a.m.	
			Own Artillery. Active all day but quiet at night	
		9pm	S.O.S. Signal on our left – next Corps front – a barrage was put up by Artillery on left, our own Artillery did not co-operate.	
			Aircraft. Our own very active all day particularly towards 11pm. A few aerial fights observed without any very definite results. An enemy M/C plane worn own lines about midnight.	
			M.G. Searching Fire – Targets P.1.C.1,2,3,4 } Rounds fired	Pro 6000
			P.1.a.2,3,4 } 6000	
		9A.	A fairly quiet day except for own Artillery who are particularly active between 11.30pm & 1am & again from 2.30 to 3.30 am. A few falling as usual in vicinity of own M.G.S.	
			Aircraft. No enemy info up at all. Very few of ours.	
			Weather. Very blustery & cloudy all day. Fairly heavy rain at night.	
			116th Bde. relieved 115th Bde. in left Sub Sector.	Horses & Mules Strength 6.45
				9.169 Mls

A6945. Wt. W14422/M1160 350,000 12/16 D. D. & L. Forms/C/2118/14

WAR DIARY or INTELLIGENCE SUMMARY

Army Form C. 2118.

Place	Date	Hour	Summary of Events and Information	Remarks and references to Appendices
HOLLEBEKE Sector.	Aug 26th		(Contd.) During day took 100,000 rounds S.A.A. up to guns. Gun limbers with six mules each. Warning order having been received from 118th Bde. re a proposed small local advance in which our batteries would cooperate –	
			M.G. Searching Fire – Targets P.i.a.3 b.4 d.3. } Rounds fired	6,000
			C. & D. Batteries 9.30 pm – 3.30 am J.31.d.1, 2 & 3 C.H. } 6,000	
	27th		Rained steadily from 11 am onwards throughout day & am exceptionally heavy downpour during night	30 Rds service nonfiring
			Artillery own & enemy quiet all day	
		8.30pm	S.O.S. Signal on our left. Both C. & D. Batteries (M.G.) opened immediately on their "NORMAL" S.O.S Target" until "O.K." signalled. Enemy artillery retaliation slight, on Battery positions without result.	
			C. Battery Target P.i.c.55, K.P.i.6.2.8 } Rds fired 2000	6750
			D. " " P.i.6.42 to J.31.d.65 } 4750	
			Searching Fire also carried out as usual 9.30pm to 3.30 am Targets P.i.8.6 & 3.d.1 } 6,000 Rds P.i.c.1.2, 3.H4	6,000
		10pm	S.O.S. Signal observed on our front, but M.G. Batteries were not asked for support	
				Strength Horses Mules 8-49 9-142 A.R.

A6945 Wt. W1422/M1160 350,000 12/16. D.D. & L. Forms/C/2118/14.

Army Form C. 2118.

WAR DIARY
or
INTELLIGENCE SUMMARY.
(Erase heading not required.)

Instructions regarding War Diaries and Intelligence Summaries are contained in F. S. Regs., Part II. and the Staff Manual respectively. Title pages will be prepared in manuscript.

Place	Date	Hour	Summary of Events and Information	Remarks and references to Appendices
HOLLEBEKE Sector	Aug 28th		The heavy downpour during night followed by a very strong gale of wind still approx (S.W.) which dried the ground up apparently. A few showers both in morning & evening. Moonlight night	
			Enemy Artillery batteries more active than usual particularly between 7 & 11.30 p.m. also after our MGs started their usual Searching fire. Enemy retaliated each time with "whizz-bangs" & so nearly found 'C' Battery that it was ordered to cease fire. Shells were dropping 50' to 100' in front of 'D' battery	
			Aircraft. Very few Bocheles out all day until evening. Several enemy M/cs observed flying over, very high towards back areas.	9.30 a arrive
			M.G. Searching fire. Targets. Roads. P1.a.3. (C Batt) Rds	
			9.30 p.m. to 3.30 a.m. C D Batteries J.31d 1,2,3 & 4	3750 3000
	29th		Heavy showers at intervals throughout day. Still very cloudy.	
			Artillery activity on both sides much as usual.	4 Horses & arrive
			Enemy M Guns firing by night from our right between 8.30 & 11.30 p.m. occasionally transversing across our battery positions without effect	
				Horses Mules 8 & 44

WAR DIARY
or
INTELLIGENCE SUMMARY
(Erase heading not required.)

Army Form C. 2118.

Place	Date	Hour	Summary of Events and Information	Remarks and references to Appendices
HOLLEBEKE Sector	Aug 29		M.G. Searching Fire - Targets O.12.d.1,2,3,4 } Rounds fired	
			C.LD. Patrons 9.30 p.m. to 3 a.m. P.1.c.1,2,3,4 }	6500
	30th		Slight improvement in weather, still cloudy with bright intervals.	6500
			Reconnoitred positions for 'C' Battery approx 800' forward in open from which they could	1 O.P. revue
			give overhead fire with safety in the event of our local advance taking place, present	
			battery position would be slightly over 2000' from proposed advance line held by infantry.	
			Enemy Artillery A good deal of Regt. bursting Shrapnel throughout day & shelling	
			chiefly on left of the CATERPILLAR TRACK particularly between 3.45 - 4.15 p.m. Own	
			artillery fairly active day & night.	
	4 p.m.		Coloured lights went up on our left Artillery active on both sides	
	10.30		11 p.m. A great number of coloured lights on our right apparently reported our	
			own S.O.S signal. Great activity artillery & M.G guns on both sides which quietened	
			down before 11.30 p.m.	
			(Re cooperation of our guns (Artillery & M.G) apparently not called for	Sgt 1st
	2 a.m.		Enemy coloured lights on our front very little activity resulted	AMSORs
				Sgt L.D. Mrs.
				8 2 145

Army Form C. 2118.

WAR DIARY
or
INTELLIGENCE SUMMARY.
(Erase heading not required.)

Place	Date	Hour	Summary of Events and Information	Remarks and references to Appendices
HOLLEBEKE Sector	Jan 30th		M.G Searching Fire - Targets P1, C2, 3, 4 Roundehoek WOODFARM area C+D Batteries 9.30p - 11am (J31. d.4) 6,500	6,500
	31st		Showery raul during day. A fine moonlight night. Enemy artillery fairly quiet on own front, with the usual amount of shelling to N of CATERPILLAR TRACK Own Artillery not quite so active as usual Aircraft were up in small numbers during evening During night several planes (enemy) were heard over own lines M.G Searching Fire - TARGETS BELGIAN WOOD Retained C+B Batteries 9.30pm - 11am J31d 1+3 6,500 J31C1	6,500 Showery etc J x 14508 Herries B J 9 24 Meets 45

WAR DIARY
~~INTELLIGENCE SUMMARY~~
(Erase heading not required.)

Place	Date	Hour	Summary of Events and Information	Remarks and references to Appendices
HOLLEBEKE SECTOR	September 1st		A fine day with occasional showers	
			General Situation Fairly quiet	
			Enemy Artillery Active in our vicinity about 9 am & again 2.30 pm	
			Aircraft Active only in the early morning	
			M.G. Searching fire Targets — P.C. 1,2,3,4	
			C.D. Batteries 9.30 pm — 14 guns Rounds fired 4,500	a b 1 c d 1 2 3 4 = 500 Pdo 6,500
		2/3	39th Bde Order No 152.	
			(a) The IX Corps will relieve X Corps on the front YPRES-COMINES Canal to J.31.a.45.15 on the night of 2nd/3rd September	
			(b) The 39th Div will relieve 24th Div on the front GRAVEYARD COTTAGE (inclusive) to S E Corner BODMIN COPSE (exc) on night 2nd/3rd September	Shrewd of Sy
			(b) 118th Inf Bde will relieve 14th Bde in SHREWSBURY FOREST Section on 2/3rd and 3/4th Sept	9.0 x 119.082 55
			(c) One Section 228 M.G.Coy in the Line will be relieved by 37th Div M.G. Coy one night Horoscope	put

228 MACHINE GUN CO.
22 8 M G Coy
Vol 3

Army Form C. 2118.

WAR DIARY
or
INTELLIGENCE SUMMARY.
(Erase heading not required.)

Instructions regarding War Diaries and Intelligence Summaries are contained in F. S. Regs., Part II. and the Staff Manual respectively. Title pages will be prepared in manuscript.

Place	Date	Hour	Summary of Events and Information	Remarks and references to Appendices
HOLLEBEKE SECTOR	2nd		of 3/4th Sept. The incoming 2 Sections arrived of 3/4th Sept. 208 M.G. Coy Reed 2 Sections were relieved 2nd Bns M.G. Coy in the line (SHREWSBURY FOREST Sect) on night of 3/4th Sept. Relief in accordance with D.O.152 above. One section of guns was relieved by 2nd M.G. Coy (3rd Bde Coy) at dawn on 2nd inst. The incoming guns of 2nd Y Coy being under O.C. 208 Coy. General Situation quiet except for a good deal of enemy snipping now and even between 6-10am. Also occasional shelling of track on S.W side of BATTLE WOOD throughout day. Aircraft (presumed enemy) very active during night M.G Searchington - Targets WOOD FARM (J21.d.5.2) Randshoes BELGIAN WOOD J.13.c.1 7,000 P.1.C. 344 Square H	S.Kennett 9.2.19.04 Jones.W BWV

Army Form C. 2118.

WAR DIARY
or
INTELLIGENCE SUMMARY.
(Erase heading not required.)

Place	Date	Hour	Summary of Events and Information	Remarks and references to Appendices
HOLLEBEKE Sector	3rd		In accordance with 39th Div Order No.152. Remaining 8 guns of 228 M.G. Coy were relieved by 247 M.G. Coy.	
			Relief was carried out by day owing to the extreme difficulty of finding ones way about at night & small parties came up independently from the BRICK STACK. Relief completed 4.45 pm	
Ref Map ZILLEBEKE Sheet 28NW4			Relief of 2nd Division. One section of 8 guns of 228 M.G. Coy relieved 24th Dist. M.G. Coy in SHREWSBURY FOREST Section. Remaining 3 Sections temporarily in reserve at RIDGE WOOD N.5.C.10.9.	
4NE3 posts of			Weather A sudden improvement. Very hot + Sunny. M.G. positions taken over from 24th Div Coy were Reserve positions R5,6,7,8 in the neighbourhood of I.29.d.7.4. SIXTY about I.29.d.7.4. Particulars of S.O.S. Targets as handed over are :-	O.80 Q 144 Horses Mules 55

Gun	Direction	Q.E.	Range	Target
R.6	103° 7 min	5° 30'	2200	J 32.a.10.60
R.7	86°	6° 50'	2400	J 26.c.40.70
R.8	108°	5° 30'	2200	J 31.d.50.45
R.5				

Army Form C. 2118.

WAR DIARY
INTELLIGENCE SUMMARY.
(Erase heading not required.)

Instructions regarding War Diaries and Intelligence Summaries are contained in F. S. Regs., Part II. and the Staff Manual respectively. Title pages will be prepared in manuscript.

Place	Date	Hour	Summary of Events and Information	Remarks and references to Appendices
HILL 60 SECTOR Refce. ZILLEBEKE 28NW4NE3	3rd		Enemy Artillery Heavily shelled Battery on left of M.G. position (T.29.d.7.4) between 6-6.30pm & continued intermittently till 8.30pm.	
			Miscellaneous Shelling at intervals throughout night	
			Own Artillery Fairly active throughout day mostly on our left at 9pm, 10pm & 12.30am	
			Aircraft was heard overhead continually from 8.30pm to 12mn	2,750
			Weather dry. Moonlight night	
			M.G. Harassing Fire Gun Position Target Roundsfired	
			Time 10pm to 1am R9 T.29.d.7.4 T.26.c.9.3 2,750	
			& T.32.b.0.2.9.0	
	4th		Fine day with light westerly wind	
			Enemy Artillery Moderate amount of shelling throughout day mostly in region of MOUNT SORREL & in valley at T.29.a & b	Strength
			One of our M Guns hit & put out of action	10.4.1914
			Own Artillery fairly active as usual with intense fire between 10-10.30am	Nooes. Inclay
				55
				B.w.4

Army Form C. 2118.

Army Form C. 2118.

WAR DIARY
or
INTELLIGENCE SUMMARY.
(Erase heading not required.)

Instructions regarding War Diaries and Intelligence Summaries are contained in F. S. Regs., Part II. and the Staff Manual respectively. Title pages will be prepared in manuscript.

Place	Date	Hour	Summary of Events and Information	Remarks and references to Appendices
HILL 60 Sector	4th		Aircraft 2 enemy observation balloons up beyond MT SORREL.	
			Planes fairly active on both sides were heard overhead about every half hour between 10.30pm & 3am.	
			Occasional enemy M/Gs flying low over our lines in evening fired at by our A.A. guns without success.	
			No.9 Harassing fire Targets. T.32 a.6.9 to 6.6 ⎱ Rounds fired	
			T.26 c.9.3 to 32 b.03.90 ⎰ 2,500	2,500
	5th		Fine day - light S.E. wind	
			Artillery rather less active than usual on both sides	
			Our artillery very active from 9-9.30am on our left	
			Aircraft enemy machines more numerous than usual again flying low over our lines engaged by our A.A. guns without visible result	
			No 9 Harassing fire - Targets T.26 c. 56.29 to 56.00 ⎱ Rounds fired	
			8.30pm - 4.30am T.26 c.90.29 to T.32 b.03.90 ⎰ 3,000	
			Anti-Aircraft M.Gs mounted by day fired in all 3,500	6,500
				RWA
				Strength
				9 off 179 ORs
				3rd Powder
				55

Army Form C. 2118.

WAR DIARY
or
INTELLIGENCE SUMMARY
(Erase heading not required.)

Instructions regarding War Diaries and Intelligence Summaries are contained in F. S. Regs., Part II. and the Staff Manual respectively. Title pages will be prepared in manuscript.

Place	Date	Hour	Summary of Events and Information	Remarks and references to Appendices
HILL 60 Sector	6th		Weather very hot during day & close time up to 5pm. Then slight rain developing into a Thunderstorm at 4pm. Clear later. Light NE wind. Enemy Artillery moderately active during day particularly on KNOLL ROAD near ZWARTELEEN at 11am. THE BLUFF & BRICK STACK area shelled during afternoon.	
28NW4 & NE3			Our Artillery Active as usual. Intense bombardment 7.20am & 4.15pm in Sector E of YPRES. Our ration party were caught by shell fire about 8am between LA CAPELLE and The VERBRANDEN ROAD. 3 mules killed. Drivers undamaged. Recce in G. officer reconnoitred with O.C. (228 Coy) for outside positions for 2 Groups (each of 16 guns) for Barrage fire during proposed operations. M.G. Harassing Fire — Targets J26.c 53.30 to 50.63 90.30 to 80.40 J32.b 03.90 to T26.0 90.30 Rounds fired 2,750	2,750
				Strength: 90+440/Rs Horses/mules 55 RWT

Army Form C. 2118.

WAR DIARY
or
INTELLIGENCE SUMMARY.
(Erase heading not required.)

Instructions regarding War Diaries and Intelligence Summaries are contained in F. S. Regs., Part II. and the Staff Manual respectively. Title pages will be prepared in manuscript.

Place	Date	Hour	Summary of Events and Information	Remarks and references to Appendices
HILL 60 Sector	7th		Weather Heavy mist at dawn very hot close later	
			General Situation very quiet day. Marked decrease in activity on both sides	
			Aircraft Not so numerous as usual. Enemy machine flying high observed at 3.30 pm	
			M.G. Harassing fire Targets T 32 a 62 90 to 65 60 } Rounds fired	
			8.30 pm to 5 am. T 32 b 03 90 to T 32 a 95 53 } 2,750	2,750
	8th		Weather Again very misty early, remaining so till about 11 am. Afterwards very close. W. wind	1 Or wounded
			Intn. Section relief during afternoon No 2 Sect relieved No 3 Sect in positions R5, 6, 7 & 8	
			O.M.G.O & O.C. Coy again reconnoitred line for Barrage positions & accommodation for gun teams. Old German concrete dug outs examined mostly water logged & filled in with rubris & filth	
			Hostile Artillery unusually quiet throughout day	Strength
			Own Artillery quiet during day. Intense bombardment on left at 9.45 pm	O 9 a 146 O.Rs
			again at 3.50 am.	Horse Mules 55
			RWG	

Army Form C. 2118.

WAR DIARY
or
INTELLIGENCE SUMMARY
(Erase heading not required.)

Place	Date	Hour	Summary of Events and Information	Remarks and references to Appendices
Hill 60 Sector	8th		M.G. Harassing fire. Targets J 26 c. 56.37 to 05 60 Rds.	8/
			J 26 c 90.37 to J 32 6 03 90	3,000
		9 pm to 4.30 am	T 26 C 53 30 to 50 42	3,000
	9th		Weather fine very hot. W. wind	
			Working Party 40 men & 4 NCOS up at 7am cleaning old German trench at T 36 to 4.8. Work was stopped by hostile shelling at about 12 midday which was directed practically on this trench & the forward slope of wood in front. Working party was transferred to T 30 C. 80 25 & started on releaning B.O.d dug outs in this vicinity. Work continued till 5.30 pm.	
			Hostile Artillery active all day. Our Artillery also very active putting up a barrage on our front 8.40 pm.	
			Own Aircraft very active. 4 fewer enemy machines observed flying high.	
			M.G. Harassing fire. Target J 26 d. 35 65 to 60 23. Rounds fired 250	250
			NOTE Guns requested to cease fire by O.C. Infantry working party laying cable in front of gun position. R.W.†	Strength Q & 146 O.R. Horses mules 55

D.D. & L., London, E.C. Sch. 82a. Forms/C/2118/14

Army Form C. 2118.

WAR DIARY
or
INTELLIGENCE SUMMARY.
(Erase heading not required.)

Place	Date	Hour	Summary of Events and Information	Remarks and references to Appendices
HILL 60 Sector	10th		Weather. 1Rest meet up to 8.30am. Very Hot later. W wind.	
			O.C. Coy up line with O.C. 110 M.G.Coy (21st Div) who are being attached to 39th	
			Div for Barrage work in forth coming operations	
			Proposed positions for guns reconnoitred & work carried on.	
			Working Party 36 men & 4 N.C.Os Realarming dug outs	
			Carrying up material from JACKSONS DUMP & building shelter for west	
			feeling & ammunition depots for barrage M Guns	
			Enemy Artillery fairly active all day Particularly shelling a battery to	
			left rear of gun positions	
			Own Artillery also active Putting up a barrage on left at 3 P.m.	
			Quiet during night until 1 am. when a barrage was put up on right	
			believed to be an organised raid by our troops	Straight
			Aircraft engaged activity Enemy flying low over our lines at 5 P.m.	90 x 1760lb Novos Amber 55
			M.G. Harassing fire Targets J.32. a,65. 48 } Rounds fired	
			J.32. b.58. 45 } 3,000	
			J.32.a.60.95 to 62.75 } 500	3,500
			Rounds fired at enemy aircraft by day	Nil

Army Form C. 2118.

WAR DIARY
or
INTELLIGENCE SUMMARY.
(Erase heading not required.)

Instructions regarding War Diaries and Intelligence Summaries are contained in F. S. Regs., Part II. and the Staff Manual respectively. Title pages will be prepared in manuscript.

Place	Date	Hour	Summary of Events and Information	Remarks and references to Appendices
HILL 60 Sector	11th		Hostile Artillery active all round HILL60 and KNOLL ROAD particularly	
			between hours 10.30-12 midday & between 2-4 pm.	
			No Harassing fire by request owing to working parties laying cable	
			in front of gun positions	
			"Weather extremely hot day.	
			Working Party as usual 9am-4:30pm. Still water pumped out from old dug	
			outs but still very foul require a good deal of cleaning	
	12th		Weather Colder - Blustery wind & cloudy	
			Hostile Artillery active during morning same areas, quietening	20 OR wounded
			afternoon & evening	Strength
			Working Party as usual 9am to 4:30 pm more material carried up from dump	90 O+144 ORs
			for overhead cover for brest firing cleaning etc. which are almost completed	Horses Mules
			No M.G. Harassing fire owing to Brigade relief ("11th Bde relieve 11th")	55
				RWT

Army Form C. 2118.

WAR DIARY
or
INTELLIGENCE SUMMARY.
(Erase heading not required.)

Instructions regarding War Diaries and Intelligence Summaries are contained in F. S. Regs., Part II. and the Staff Manual respectively. Title pages will be prepared in manuscript.

Place	Date	Hour	Summary of Events and Information	Remarks and references to Appendices
HILL 60 Sector	13th		Our Artillery active all day.	11
			Enemy Artillery very active at intervals notably 9.30am 3pm round our gun positions. At 6.45pm a direct hit was obtained on M.G of 17th Sherwoods & the Colonel killed.	
			11.45pm H.E. & Gas shells were sent over & bombardment continued till dawn	
			Aerial activity very slight - all enemy M.Gs firing Rifle	
			M.G Harassing fire - Target T.26.c.56.37 Roundsfired	
			9pm to 4.30am to T.26.c.90.34 3,000	3,000
			Working Party. Work carried on from 9am to 4.30pm on emplacements & shelters	
			Artillery activity on both sides much as usual	Reinforcement
			Work on emplacements etc 9am to 4pm - 35 men	(1 Officer)
			M.G Harassing fire Target "C" Roundsfired	
	14th		9pm to 5am T.32.a.2.3. & 9.3 12,000	12,000
			NOTE. From the night of 14/15th H.M. guns of the Div. M.G Coy. & ½ guns of the M.G Coy from the Bde in line will be engaged in Harrassing by day & night Target carefully allotted after a close study of latest Intelligence & Aerial Photos. Rate of fire will be 3,500 rounds per gun every 24 hrs until night of 17/18th when it will be increased to 5,000 rounds per gun.	Strength 10 + 194 Horses/mules 55.

Army Form C. 2118.

12

WAR DIARY
or
INTELLIGENCE SUMMARY.
(Erase heading not required.)

Place	Date	Hour	Summary of Events and Information	Remarks and references to Appendices
HILL 60 Sector	15th		Note In accordance with Instructions (GE 9(4) 2 more guns sent up to Reserve positions to fire in conjunction with Artillery during Practice Barrage	
			Enemy retaliated fairly vigorously in a miscellaneous manner up to 2:30 p.m. but there was little reply to # Barrage at 4 p.m. & he was fairly quiet during night	
			Own M.G's Cooperated in Practice Barrage. Rounds fired	
			Time 8 am to 9 am Target (c) J.32.a.2.3.t.9.3 1,500 (4 guns)	31,500
			4 p.m. to 9 p.m. Same area 12,000 (6 guns)	
			M.G Harassing fire as above + J.32.a.8.7 12,000 (4 guns)	
			(9 p.m. to 5 am)	
	16th		Working Party as usual 9am to 4pm. one of the dug-outs being quite inhabitable, a big officers was started upon to hold 15-20 men.	
			Practice Barrage 10 am & 6 pm. Target Rds fired	Strength
			Working Party as usual - during day J.26.a.65.45 to J.26.c.50.40 10,500	100. M4 M.G.
			Own M.G. Cooperated in Barrage 10 am - to 10.51 J.32.a.80.40 + J.32.a.70.30 10,500	Horses Mules
			6 p.m. - 6.54	55
				R.W.G

Army Form C. 2118.

WAR DIARY
or
INTELLIGENCE SUMMARY.
(Erase heading not required.)

Instructions regarding War Diaries and Intelligence Summaries are contained in F. S. Regs., Part II. and the Staff Manual respectively. Title pages will be prepared in manuscript.

Place	Date	Hour	Summary of Events and Information	Remarks and references to Appendices
HILL TOP Sector	16th		M.G. Harassing fire 9pm-5am J.32.a.2.3 to 9.3 Rds fired 9,000	
			J.32.b.6.6 to 6.9 3,000	33,000.
	17th		Practice Barrage by own Artillery + M.Gs 5.30am-6.30am. Retaliation on usual line	
			re forward slope near IMAGE CRESCENT (T.30.b+d) also on NE corner of FUSILIER	
			WOOD + tracks near gun positions	
				Rounds fired
			M.G. Cooperation 5.30-6.30 am Target J.26.6545 to C.5040 13,500	24,500
			Harassing fire 8.30pm-7am - Square J.26.d (Central) 11,000	
			Working Party, 2 Sections with 10 guns + equipment moved up to Battle Positions about	
			area around J.B.2 & 4.8	
	18th		T.30.C.9.3 carried on with work at gun positions when possible during day	
			Practice Barrage as before 6am-7am and 8.30 to 9.30pm. Retaliation not so vigorous	
			as usual but on same lines + with Reserve shells Tracks shelled during night	
			M.G. Cooperation intense fire carried on from Harassing fire previous night. During	Strength
			day 4 guns fired at irregular intervals on same target. 9,000 rds.	10 + 19 ot
			Enemy shelled ZWARTELEEN area + vicinity of Reserve gun positions 10am - 12 MD	Horses, mules
			at 8pm 4 of Reserve guns moved up from J.29.d to Battle Positions + carried out	55
			Harassing fire from vicinity T.30.C.9.2 at irregular intervals throughout the 24 hrs	
			ending 8pm 19th Target J.32.b.central Rounds fired	
			J.26.d.4.2 20,000	29,000.

Army Form C. 2118.

WAR DIARY
or
INTELLIGENCE SUMMARY.
(Erase heading not required.)

Place	Date	Hour	Summary of Events and Information	Remarks and references to Appendices
HILL 60 Sector	18th		Firing also included intense fire during Practice Barrage (8.30pm – 9.30pm)	
			Battery Commanders moved up to Battle positions 12 midday to make final preparations	
	19th		Ordered to be a "Silent day". All movement to be cut down to a minimum. See Orders appendix Nos 1, 2 & 3	V Appendix V 1,2,3
			All remaining guns & equipment in position by 9am → for operation Orders	
			Final improvements to gun positions made during night	
	20th		ATTACK DAY ZERO HOUR 5.40am	
			See 16 guns of Group IV opened promptly, fired as per report →	V Appendix No. 4
			Retaliation & enemy barrage at first fell on forward slope about 200' in front of	
			Battery positions about IMAGE CRESCENT, but later the crest occupied by	
			batteries was shelled continuously throughout operation	
			They appeared to pay special attention to duck board tracks on our right &	
			left flanks. Guns on right flank had an uncomfortable time & had two	Strength
			emplacements knocked in but guns undamaged.	Q OR 10.174
			Later in the day shelling seemed to come from COMINES direction.	Horses/mules 55

Army Form C. 2118.

WAR DIARY
or
INTELLIGENCE SUMMARY.
(Erase heading not required.)

Instructions regarding War Diaries and Intelligence Summaries are contained in F. S. Regs., Part II. and the Staff Manual respectively. Title pages will be prepared in manuscript.

Place	Date	Hour	Summary of Events and Information	Remarks and references to Appendices
HILL 60 Sector	20th		Situation Apparently most of our objective taken, but Div on left held up	
			Slightly a 2nd attack made by this Division at 6.19 p.m.	
			Our S O S signal went up 7.25 p.m.	
			Very dark night	
	21st		A fine day.	
			"Precautionary Barrage" fired by Artillery & M. G. at 4.30 a.m.	
			Div on left again attacked "GREEN LINE" 9.30 a.m. with Art. & M.G. support	
			Total Rounds fired on 20th/21st - 323,000	323,000 V. Appendix No 7
	22nd		8.25 a.m. One of our dug outs hit by own Artillery. 4 killed & 9 wounded	14 OR killed 11 OR wounded 2. Reinforcements
			Heavy bombardment throughout night from direction of COMINES on our dug outs & track to N. of our positions	Strength O OR 10 764 Horses/mules 55

RWS

Army Form C. 2118.

WAR DIARY
or
INTELLIGENCE SUMMARY.
(Erase heading not required.)

Place	Date	Hour	Summary of Events and Information	Remarks and references to Appendices
HILL 60 Sector	23rd		Received instructions with regard to relief by 111 M.G. Coy (37th Div) at 9.10 am "Guides to be at BUS HOUSE 9am"	
			1st Section arrived at positions about 11.30am. Relief complete about 3pm	OR 1 Killed & 5 Wounded
			Intermittent shelling all round tracks & approaches to gun positions most of day	
	24th		Coy back to new HQ at RIDGE WOOD	
			A quiet day at RIDGE WOOD. Men need a good rest after strenuous work carried on continuously since 10th inst	
	25th		Very Wet day. In preparation for offensive operations starting tomorrow, 228 M.G. Coy relieved 238 M.G. Coy (41st Div) in CLONMEL COPSE	Strength 10 × 158 ORs Horses/Mules 55
			Coy left RIDGE WOOD complete with guns 9.30am	
			Relief complete by 12.30 noon — for operation orders see →	appendix No. 5.
				RWT

Army Form C. 2118.

WAR DIARY
or
INTELLIGENCE SUMMARY
(Erase heading not required.)

Instructions regarding War Diaries and Intelligence Summaries are contained in F. S. Regs., Part II. and the Staff Manual respectively. Title pages will be prepared in manuscript.

Place	Date	Hour	Summary of Events and Information	Remarks and references to Appendices
HILL 60 Sector	26th		ATTACK DAY ZERO HOUR 5.50 a.m. All guns of Group II opened promptly with own Artillery & fired as per separate report p.c.s. →	Wounded. 2 o/R. 2 mules
			Retaliation on the whole was weak, hostile barrage falling at various forward slope about 450ʸ in front of Battery positions	Appendix No 6.
			Miscellaneous shelling continued all day in vicinity of gun positions also HEDGE ST. + CANADA TUNNELS. Special attention being paid to duck board tracks	
			Communication with O.C. Coy. & D.M.G.O. at HEDGE ST TUNNELS was well maintained throughout	
			Best feeling was done entirely by hand, at times it was only just possible to keep pace with the demand by utilising all runners & orderlies etc.	Strength 0 O/R 10 + 156
			Guns fired well throughout – Slight trouble with "Puno fixing collar roller"	Horses/mules 53

Army Form C. 2118.

Army Form C. 2118.

WAR DIARY
or
INTELLIGENCE SUMMARY.
(Erase heading not required.)

Place	Date	Hour	Summary of Events and Information	Remarks and references to Appendices
HILL 60 Sector	26th		A quiet night after S.O.S signal at 8.10 pm	1 OR wounded
	27		Abnormally quiet up to 6.40 pm when SOS signal went up. Enemy Barrage very intense but in front of battery position. Both sides very active till about 9.30 pm after that a quiet night	appendix No 6 237/000
	28.		S.O.S signal up at 1 am Ael guns fired as per seperate report. Totalrounds fired 26th–28th 237,000. Relieved by 247 M.G Coy (31 Division) - Guides 12 midday at BUS HOUSE Tripods & belt boxes exchanged with incoming Coy. Company left RIDGE WOOD & was conveyed by Mootor bus to the BERTHEN area. Billeted at farm house about R 22 b 45. Very comfortable & accomodation exactly suitable for a M.G Coy with transport. 1st bus load arrived about 6 pm. 2nd lot about 9 pm.	Strength 9 + 155 Horses & mules 53 RWT

Army Form C. 2118.

19

WAR DIARY
or
INTELLIGENCE SUMMARY.
(Erase heading not required.)

Place	Date	Hour	Summary of Events and Information	Remarks and references to Appendices
BERTHEN AREA	29th		A fine day. Gave the men a rest, doing little work beyond cleaning guns, inspecting clothing & equipment	Strength O 0 10 9 155 Horses, mules 53.
	30th		Another fine day. Exchange of clothing, fueling of beets, washing & repairing limbers	

228 Co. M.G. Corps

Appendix No. 1

M.G. Instructions
in connection with 39th Division Order No.153
issued by Capt. J.R. Royds.

Ref: Maps
SHREWSBURY FOREST
1/10.000
ZILLEBEKE 28 NW & NE
1/10,000

Organisation — 228 M.G. Coy will form Group II consisting of 2 Batteries "C" & "D" each composed of 8 guns

Idea — To Co-operate with Barrage fire, by supporting the attack on each objective & firing a protective barrage beyond after each objective has been captured.

Disposition — The right battery ("C") will be formed by Nos 1 & 2 Sections, which will be known as C right and left Sub-batteries respectively. Similarly 3 & 4 Sections will form "D" battery

Frontage — Each battery will have a frontage of 85"

Location — "C" Battery right flank I.30.c.95.05
            "D"   "   left   "   I.30.c.94.35

Centres of Sub-batteries
"C" Rt Sub battery No 1   I.30.c. 95.09
"C" Left   do   . 2   .   95.18
"D" Rt.   do   . 3   .   95.26
"D" Left   do   . 4   .   96.34

Group Commander — (O.C. 228 M.G.Coy.) will be dug out approx I.30.c. 95.35.

Composition — 228 M.G. Coy with 16 guns will form GROUP No.2.
Each section of 4 guns will be commanded by an officer & each battery of 8 guns by a Battery Commander who will be in telephonic Communication with the Group Commander & will receive all orders thro' him.

P.T.O.

II

Commanders

"C" Battery	No. 1 Section	No. 2 Section
2nd Lt. Usher	2nd Lt. Thorburn	2nd Lt. Aldridge

"D" Battery	No. 3 Section	No. 4 Section
2nd Lt. Yule	2nd Lt. Hawkins	2nd Lt. Whitehead

Communication — Group Commander will be in communication with D.M.G.O. at Bde. H.Q. by buried cable.

Battery Commanders will make their own arrangements for conveyance of orders to their Sub-batteries.

Firing — Details of Barrage Targets and S.A.A. to be expended on each target, are issued on Separate Instructions

Section Commanders will satisfy themselves that all guns & fighting equipment is in good order & that arrangements for belt filling, water & oil supply etc., are satisfactory.

Belt Filling — One shelter per 4 guns has been erected at from 50 to 80ˣ behind gun positions. 2 Belt filling M/Cs. will be set up in 2 of these shelters for "C" Battery & 2 in dug outs near "D" battery. The remaining shelters will be used for belt filling by hand.

Water (for guns). There will be 2 Petrol Tins at each gun position

Runners — Each section will have at least one runner thoroughly acquainted with the following positions:-

```
LARCH WOOD TUNNELS   (D.M.G.O)
Repairs Depot & Dump.   I.29d.83.50
     Ammunition -       I.29d.50.40
```

P.T.O.

III.

Spare Parts — Only those parts absolutely necessary will be taken to gun emplacements. One set of spare parts per pair of guns to be deposited in Coy dug-out.

Personnel — At the guns will be kept down to the absolute minimum, viz. 2 men per gun, 2 N.C.O's per section one of whom is to be in charge of belt filling & just those men deemed necessary by S.O. for belt filling.

Work — After 16th inst no work of any description will be carried on in the open by daylight. All emplacements & other new work to be carefully camouflaged by day & rendered absolutely in-conspicuous.

Movement to & from dug outs etc. to be reduced to a minimum.

Parties of Infantry to be prevented as far as possible from passing by gun positions.

Aircraft — On approach of hostile Aircraft everyone will either take cover from view or remain absolutely stationary.

Movement will be notified later.

Appendix K.

Barrage.

Battery	Gun	No.I Range	V.I	Q.E	True Bearing	No.II Range	V.I	Q.E	True Bearing	No.III Range	V.I	Q.E	True Bearing	No.IV Range	V.I	Q.E	True Bearing
"C"	1	1545	20	1°43	100	1925	24	3°8	98	2150	25	4°20	98	2350	25	5°40	102
(No.1 Section)	2	1585	18	1°50	98½	1940	24	3°10	97	2160	25	4°24	94	2345	25	5°50	101
	3	1600	15	2°0	97	1955	23	3°18	96	2190	25	4°28	96	2395	24	6°0	100
	4	1625	15	2°3	95½	1990	22	3°22	95	2190	25	4°36	95	2420	23	6°12	99
(No.2 Section)	5	1630	15	2°8	94	1990	23	3°30	94	2200	25	4°40	94	2440	21	6°28	98
	6	1645	14	2°12	92½	2010	24	3°32	93	2220	25	4°48	93	2460	20	6°36	94
	7	1660	13	2°18	91	2030	25	3°40	92	2240	25	4°52	91½	2480	19	6°51	96
	8	1675	12	2°22	89	2050	25	3°45	91	2250	25	5°0	90	2500	18	7°0	95
"D"	9	1690	12	2°18	89½	2050	25	3°45	89	2250	25	4°20	90	2500	19	6°58	96
(No.3 Section)	10	1670	13	2°20	88	2050	24	3°48	88	2160	25	4°25	89	2525	18	7°10	95
	11	1690	14	2°38	86½	2065	22	3°50	87	2180	25	4°30	88	2550	17	7°25	94
	12	1710	15	2°25	85	2050	20	3°55	86	2200	25	4°40	87	2545	17	7°36	93
(No.4 Section)	13	1735	15	2°30	83½	2050	20	3°56	85	2290	25	4°44	86	2600	16	7°50	92
	14	1750	14	2°38	82	2060	20	4°0	84	2210	24	4°48	85	2620	15	8°2	90
	15	1780	13	2°50	80½	2065	20	4°0	83	2210	23	4°50	84	2640	15	8°15	90
	16	1800	12½	2°55	79	2045	20	4°11	82	2220	22	—	83	2650	15	8°30	89

Note: All bearings are True. Creep barrages to the right.

228. M.G. Coy.   Appendix. #3

Instructions for Barrage Fire
in connection with Div. Order No.163
of 18/9/17

Group II

1. Targets & rates of firing will be as in Table "A"
amended Copy 18/9/17 of Divl Instructions No. 4.
(One copy has been issued to each Battery & Section
Commander)

2. Direction & Elevation for each gun will be as laid
down in Appendix No.2, for the 4 Successive
Barrages. Except that guns will fire in pairs at
the same Q.E, so that only two different elevations
will be used in any one Section of 4 guns.
(Copies issued to Batt'y & Section Commanders)

3. Battery & Section Commanders will make all
necessary arrangements whereby fire may be
switched on to any of the 250° squares (enumerated
in appendix No.3) by any or all of the guns under
their command & immediately, on receipt of the
order giving the square reference number.
(Copies app. 3. issued to Batty. & Section Commanders)

4. Compasses will be carefully checked & any
variations duly noted.

5. Watches will be synchronised at the H.Q of Bny.
in the line. (LARCHWOOD TUNNELS) at 4 pm daily.

6. S.O.S. Signal in the event of S.O.S. after operations
both batteries will open fire on their final
barrage lines, at the rate of one belt per gun in
2 minutes for 10 minutes & thereafter 50 rounds per
min. until situation is clear.

7. Laying the Gun. All the usual precautions when
using Indirect Overhead fire will be taken.
Tripods to be firmly bedded down & laying checked
after every 50 rounds.

8. Belt Filling. N.C.O's in charge of ammunition
depots will each have a list showing the rate of
firing & filling of belts required.

9. All Nos 1 & N.C.O's on the gun should have an
accurate Knowledge of Q.E. & direction for each
barrage & rate of firing.
This should be memorised as far as possible.

10. **Hostile Aircraft**

One m.gun per battery will be detailed to switch off its Barrage line of fire & engage any enemy plane which may come within close range.

At this stage of operations it is of the utmost importance to prevent enemy machines getting sufficiently close to our lines to obtain valuable information & photographs

The guns detailed for Defence against enemy aircraft will invariably open fire at suitable targets & any failure to comply with this order will be treated as a case for disciplinary action.

Appendix 4

Report of Firing done by Machine Guns of 228 Machine Gun Coy during offensive operations commencing at 5.40 am the 20/9/17.

	TARGET	TIME	ROUNDS	REMARKS
1.	J.32a. 00.40 to J.26c. 30.20	5.40 - 5.43	4000	I Barrage
2.	J.32a. 70.40 J.26d. 00.15	5.43 - 6.0	18,000	II Barrage
3.	J.32.b 15.30 J.26d 40.20	6.0 - 7.0	50,000	III
4.	J.32b 50.00 to 90.80	7.0 - 10.15	115,000	Final Barrage on S.O.S Line
(a)	Enemy Concentrating	12.28 to 1 p.m.	6,000	"C" Battery
(b)	Supporting attack by Div on left	6.19 - 6.49 pm	33,000	"C" & "D" 15 guns
(c)	S.O.S Signal	7.25 - 8 pm	26,000	—
21/9/17 (d)	Precautionary Barrage	am am 4.30 - 4.46	6,000	"D" Battery S.O.S. line & beyond
(e)	Support attack by Div on left	am am 9.30 - 10.0	31,000	"C" & "D" S.O.S line
(f)	S.O.S line	pm pm 4.30 - 5.30	12,000	S.O.S line
(g)	Practice Barrage	pm pm 7.0 to 7.15	22,000	S.O.S line

Total Rounds. 323,000

Appendix No 5

Operation Orders
(in accordance with S.O. 106)

Issued by Capt J A Rayds

Ref^ce Maps: Shrewsbury Forest 1/10,000
Zillebeke 28NW3, NE3

The 39th Division will attack the GREEN LINE from J26 d 79 to J21 6 4215 on K day

The 33rd Div will be on the left

118 Bde with attack on the right

The 116 Bde on the left

228 MG Coy & 123 MG Coy (41st Div) will cooperate with Barrage fire

116 & 118 MG Coy will accompany their respective Brigades

Organisation MG Companies engaged in Barrage fire will each form a Group Composed of 2 Batteries each consisting of 8 guns

Composition 228 MG Coy will form Group I composed of C & D Batteries
Group Commander Lieut Fyffe

C Battery { No 1 Section 2/Lt Shaw
           { No 2   "   Aldridge
D Battery { No 3   "   Hawkins
           { No 4   "   Lishers

The Senior Section Commander in each Battery will act as Battery Commander

Barrages Both Groups will support the attack by bringing intense fire to bear on JOIST TRENCH & TOWER TRENCH later placing a barrage on the reverse slopes of the TOWER HAMLETS SPUR & finally placing a barrage 500' beyond our final objective which will be the No 5 Barrage line

II

The attack will also be supported by a M G Barrage by 19th Div on the line J.26.d.60 - J.27.d.64

SOS — In the event of the signal going up after operations all MGs will open on their final barrage lines at the rate of one belt per gun in 2 minutes for 10 min & thereafter 40 rds per min until situation clears.

Firing — Time table giving periods of firing & rate will be as in Table "A" (Instructions No 1) issued in connection with Div O No 166. Copy of this table to be in possession of each section & Battery Commander.

Location — Centre of "C" Battery   Centre of "D" Battery
J 19 C 40 15   J 19 C 42 28

Switching — Calculations will be prepared beforehand to enable any or all of the guns to switch on to any Target Square at a moments notice.

Personnel — at gun positions will be reduced to a minimum while taking into consideration the rate of belt filling necessary to keep guns going.

Watches — will be synchronised at Bde HQ in the line at 5.15 pm daily.

Laying of Guns — to be checked after every 50 rounds. New Barrels only will be used & special attention given to the stability of Mounting.
NCOs:- No 1 will be thoroughly conversant with the various Q E & times of lift.

Communication — Any lines laid to or from Group I HQ will be tested every 10 minutes for breakages etc.

III

Repair Shop will be established at LARK ROW TUNNEL

Runners 1 Runner per section of 4 guns will be detailed & will remain at Coy HQ. They will be used for belt filling whenever possible.
2 Runners to remain with O.C. Coy at No 2 LARK ROW in HEDGE ST TUNNELS (H.Q. of DMGC)

Ration Party will be found from Reserve men at RIDGE WOOD, who will be responsible for bringing rations up to gun positions.

Appendix No. 6

Report of firing done by Machine Guns of 228 Machine Gun Coy during offensive operations commencing 5.50 am 26/9/17.

TIME	TARGET	ROUNDS	REMARKS
5.50 am	J.27a. 35.60 to 21c. 85.45	4000	I Barrage line
5.52 am	J.27.b. 18.25 to 21d. 40.47	19,500	II do
6.1 am	J.27.b. 60.20 to 21d. 95.45	20,000	III do
6.20 am to 7.20 am	Same Target	26,500	III (or final)
11 am to 11.30 am	Square J.33.a.3 J.33.a.2	4,500 4,000	Do. occasional bursts 4 guns of C Battery 4 " D "
12.40 pm	S.O.S. lines	14,000	Half guns - 1 Belt in 10 min.
2 pm to 2.30 pm	Left of S.O.S. line + 200x Square J.33.b.1 J.33.a.2	3,000 2,500 2500	4 guns of D Batt. 4 " C " 4 " D "
6.10 pm - 7.40	S.O.S Signal	32,000	All guns
8.10 pm	S.O.S. Signal	15,500	All guns for 25 min
27/9/17 5. am	S.O.S. lines	33,500	6 wm Art Barrage S.O.S
6.40 pm	S.O.S. Signal	10,000	S.O.S on left
7.25 pm	do	31,000	Fired for 35 min
28/9/17 1 am	S.O.S Signal	11,500	All guns

Total Rounds 234,000

No 39th Division

[Stamp: No. 228 MACHINE GUN COY. ORDERLY ROOM Date 2/11/17 MACHINE GUN CORPS]

Herewith War Diary for
October 1917 Original Copy

_____ Capt.,
Comdg. No. 228 Machine Gun Coy

66

War Diary.

from 1st October 1914 – 31st October 1914.

Vol. 4.

Army Form C. 2118.

WAR DIARY
or
INTELLIGENCE SUMMARY.
(Erase heading not required.)

Instructions regarding War Diaries and Intelligence Summaries are contained in F. S. Regs., Part II. and the Staff Manual respectively. Title pages will be prepared in manuscript.

Place	Date	Hour	Summary of Events and Information	Remarks and references to Appendices
BERTHEN AREA	Oct 1st		Parades: 9am to 12.30pm Inspection - P.T. - Gun Drill - I.A. - Box Respirator Drill	Reinforcements 12 ORs
			Weather: Heavy rain in evening	Reinforcements 12 ORs
	2nd		Parades: 8.30am to 12.30pm as usual	
			Rest Camp 5 ORs to Rest Camp - Bailleul Station 8am	
	3rd		Parades: 8.30am to 12.30pm as usual	Reinforcements 30 ORs
			Weather: Fine	(30 ORs Reinforcements) 39th Division
	4th		Parades: 8.30am to 12.30pm - as usual. Preparation for inspection by GOC 39th Division	Strength of Coy 10 + 198
			Weather: Drill - Heavy rain in evening	

Army Form C. 2118.

WAR DIARY
or
INTELLIGENCE SUMMARY.
(Erase heading not required.)

Place	Date	Hour	Summary of Events and Information	Remarks and references to Appendices
BERTHEN AREA	5th		Preliminary inspection etc. By Major General Feetham commanding 39th Division. The company were highly complimented by the GOC on their past work, especially on July 31st, Sept 20th and 26th	
			Course of Instruction: 1 N.C.O	
			Weather. Heavy showers at 1:30 pm – dull	
	6th		Church Service C of E at BERTHEN Church Army Hut	
			Parades as usual including revolver practice	
			Weather – Showery	
	7th	am 8:55	Church Service. Non–Conformist at billet	
		am 9:55	Parades. Gas demonstration to whole company	
			Pack saddlery drill	

S.Knight + Co
10.5.44.

69A

Army Form C. 2118.

3

WAR DIARY
or
INTELLIGENCE SUMMARY.
(Erase heading not required.)

Instructions regarding War Diaries and Intelligence Summaries are contained in F.S. Regs., Part II. and the Staff Manual respectively. Title pages will be prepared in manuscript.

Place	Date	Hour	Summary of Events and Information	Remarks and references to Appendices
BERTHEN AREA	October 7th	Time	All watches and clocks put back one hour at 1am	
		Weather	Rain	
	8th	Parades	6.30am to 7.30am — 8.30am to 12.30pm — 2pm to 3pm	
		Weather	Rain	
	9th	Parades	Route march 9am to 12.30pm (9 miles) 2pm foot inspection — 2.30 to 3.30pm Stripping & cleaning guns	
		Weather	Fine	
	10th	Parades	6.30am to 3.0pm — no mid-day meal	Shergld/9Cav 10.4.14
		Weather	Heavy rain in morning — dull	

D. D. & L., London, E.C.
(M1049) Wt W17771/M2931 750,000 5/17 Sch 58 Forms/C2118/14

Army Form C. 2118.

WAR DIARY
or
INTELLIGENCE SUMMARY.
(Erase heading not required.)

Instructions regarding War Diaries and Intelligence Summaries are contained in F.S. Regs., Part II. and the Staff Manual respectively. Title pages will be prepared in manuscript.

Place	Date	Hour	Summary of Events and Information	Remarks and references to Appendices
BERTHEN AREA	11th		Parades: 6.30 am to 12.45 pm - as usual. 3 pm football match versus 116 M.G. Coy. Weather: Fair - Raining in evening	
	12th		Parades: 6.30 am to 3.30 pm - as usual. Revolver practice by sections (12 rds per man) Weather: Fair. Warning order received re relief of 34th Division	
	13th		Parades: 6.30 am to 3.30 pm - as usual. Weather: Raining heavily all morning. Church Service C. of E. at Berthen Church Army Hut 8.40 am	Strength of Coy 10 & 144

Army Form C. 2118.

WAR DIARY
or
INTELLIGENCE SUMMARY.
(Erase heading not required.)

Place	Date	Hour	Summary of Events and Information	Remarks and references to Appendices
BERTHEN AREA	14th		Church Service. Non Conformists at billets Parades 8.30am to 3pm as usual Rest Camp 2 Offrs and 10 OR to Base Depot Weather Fair Relief postponed till 15/16th	
	15		Parades 6.30am to 3.30pm as usual 1 N.C.O. to Base Depot for U.K. course Weather Fair 39th Divl Order No. 145 1) The 39th Division (less Artillery) will relieve the 34th Division (less Artillery) in the TOWER HAMLETS section on the night 15/16 October 1917 2) a) 116th Bde (less M.G. Coy and T.M.B.) will relieve the 63rd Infantry Brigade (less M.G. Coy and T.M.B.) and 2 Battalions 111 Bde by October 16th 1917 - 4am b) M.G. Coy + T.M.B relief will be carried out on the 16th Oct and night	Strength of Coy 10 + 196

Army Form C. 2118.

WAR DIARY
or
INTELLIGENCE SUMMARY.
(Erase heading not required.)

Place	Date	Hour	Summary of Events and Information	Remarks and references to Appendices
BERTHEN AREA	15th		16/17 October. Barrage M.G. Batteries will be relieved by the 228th M.G. Coy (less 8 guns) and 8 guns of the M.G. Coy of the Infantry Brigade in Divl Reserve. 8 Guns 228 M.G. Coy will be in Divl Reserve at their Transport Lines (N q d central) M.G. Relief by D.M.G.O. In accordance with 39th Divl Order 145 2) 8 guns 228 M.G. Coy and 8 guns 119th M.G. Coy will relieve 111 M.G. Coy in Barrage Battery Positions on 16th October as follows:— 'A' Battery (J 25 B 3 & 4) 4 guns 119th M.G. Coy 'B' " (J 25 a 6.3) 4 guns 119th M.G. Coy 'D' " (J 25 a 4.8) 8 guns 228th M.G. Coy 3.(a) The 8 guns 119 M.G. Coy in 'A' 'B' Battery Positions will be under the command of O.C. 228th M.G. Coy for tactical purposes.	6/

Army Form C. 2118.

WAR DIARY
or
INTELLIGENCE SUMMARY.
(Erase heading not required.)

Place	Date	Hour	Summary of Events and Information	Remarks and references to Appendices
BERTHEN AREA	15		39th Bde Order 195 (Contd). MG Relief 4(a) Guides from 111th Inf. Bde. Coy will be at VERBRANDEN CROSS ROADS T 28 a 9.5 at 3 pm 16th Coy. D9dg9t0 HEDGE ST TUNNELS. See operation Order Ap. No 1	
TOWER HAMLETS SECTOR	16th		Move - No 1 & 2 Sections, HQ proceeded to line by Motor Lorries 12.30 pm Debussing at T 32 d 9.4 - Good relief - no casualties Remainder of Company and Transport marched to N 9 d. Central at 12.30 pm. Weather Rain - very dark night MGs own Harassing fire behind S.O.S line with 2 guns during night Tank do puis too Artillery + Hostile. Heavy Recce fire near battery positions Own Active	1000 1000

/ 8 /

Army Form C. 2118.

WAR DIARY
or
INTELLIGENCE SUMMARY.
(Erase heading not required.)

Instructions regarding War Diaries and Intelligence Summaries are contained in F. S. Regs., Part II. and the Staff Manual respectively. Title pages will be prepared in manuscript.

Place	Date	Hour	Summary of Events and Information	Remarks and references to Appendices
TOWER HAMLETS Sector	14		Inef company in Bde Reserve - Cleared & straightened new camp at H.Q. & central Weather Fine but cold in morning, dark & wet night Artillery Hostile intermittent - Ammunition Carrying party caught 1 man badly wounded Guns Active General Situation Normal - quiet during night	4,000
	18		S.O.S. barrage at 5.30 a.m. own guns Co-operated Rapid fire Weather Fine Artillery Enemy Active on duckboard tracks & HEDGE ST Own Active M.G.s Enemy Harassing during night at long intervals Own Harassing during night special targets Total rds fired 6,000 1 O.R. wounded	6,000

WAR DIARY
or
INTELLIGENCE SUMMARY.
(Erase heading not required.)

Army Form C. 2118.

Place	Date	Hour	Summary of Events and Information	Remarks and references to Appendices
TOWER HAMLETS Sector	19th		39th Divisional Order No 146	
			3.(c) M.G. Company relief will be carried out on the 20th and night of 20/21st October	
			Addendum to above	
			(1) 8 guns of 118th M.G. Company will relieve the 8 guns of 114th M.G. Coy on their present battery positions	
			(2) Relief will take place by daylight on 20th and on completion the 8 guns of 118th M.G. Coy will come under orders of O.C. 228 M.G. Coy tactically.	
			(4) 116 M.G. Coy on relief will be in Divl Reserve	
			Weather Dull, Showery	
			Artillery Active on both sides	
			General Situation Normal	
				1 OR wounded

Army Form C. 2118.

WAR DIARY
or
INTELLIGENCE SUMMARY.
(Erase heading not required).

Instructions regarding War Diaries and Intelligence Summaries are contained in F. S. Regs., Part II. and the Staff Manual respectively. Title pages will be prepared in manuscript.

Place	Date	Hour	Summary of Events and Information	Remarks and references to Appendices
TOWER HAMLETS Sector	20		Relief of No. 3 & 4 Sections relieve No. 1 & 2 Section in present battery position - 8am (1 & 2 Sections to CReap Camp)	
			Weather: Fine	
			Artillery Hostile: Quiet during morning. Position heavily shelled at 3.15pm	
			Own: Active during day - quiet during night	1000
			Aircraft Hostile: Active in evening	
			Own: Very active all day	
			M.G. Hostile: Harassing during night	
			Own: Harassing during night. Targets about T.27 D.4.9 and T.27 D.4.9. 1000 rds fired	
	21st		Weather: Fine	
			Situation Normal	
			Artillery own - Very active. Hostile - active on duckboard tracks etc	
			General Situation: Normal	
			Artillery Both: Active	1000
	22nd		M.G.s Own: Harassing during night. Targets at 20 ok - 1000 rds	Strength of Coy 10 4 190

Army Form C. 2118.

WAR DIARY
or
INTELLIGENCE SUMMARY.
(Erase heading not required.)

Instructions regarding War Diaries and Intelligence Summaries are contained in F. S. Regs., Part II. and the Staff Manual respectively. Title pages will be prepared in manuscript.

Place	Date	Hour	Summary of Events and Information	Remarks and references to Appendices
TOWER HAMLET Sector	23		39th Divisional Order No. 174	
			1. (b) The 39th Division will be relieved by the 7th Div in the TOWER HAMLETS sector on the 24/25th October	
			(c) On relief 39th Div will be in close reserve behind the 7th Division and be prepared to take over the bottom front immediately after the operation	
			5 a) M.G. relief will be carried out on the night 23/24 Oct and 24th October. arrangements between DMGO's concerned	
			b) 228th M.G. Coy will be withdrawn to its Transport Lines (N9 d 8 5) on relief	
			Operation Orders (a) by Capt J. A. Roydo Comdg 228 M.G. Coy (Appendix 2)	
			1.) 8 guns of 228 M.G. Coy & 8 guns of 116 M.G. Coy will be relieved by 16 guns of 116 M.G. Coy during the day of 24th October	
			b) Range of Camp On relief Coy will proceed to CARNARVON CAMP (M 10 B 9 9)	
			Weather Fine rain	
			General Situation Normal	
			Artillery Both Active	

Army Form C. 2118.

WAR DIARY
or
INTELLIGENCE SUMMARY.
(Erase heading not required.)

Instructions regarding War Diaries and Intelligence Summaries are contained in F. S. Regs., Part II. and the Staff Manual respectively. Title pages will be prepared in manuscript.

Place	Date	Hour	Summary of Events and Information	Remarks and references to Appendices
TOWER HAMLETS Sector	2nd		**Move** — Coy to vacate CHEAP CAMP (N9 d central) and move to CARNARVON CAMP (M10 b 1.3) by noon. Remainder of company not in line and transport moved off 10.15 am marching via KEMMEL – LA CLYTTE – CANADA CORNER and RENINGHELST Rd. Arrived at new camp about noon and generally cleaned up. The company arrive complete about 7 pm from the line. Good relief – no casualties. **General Situation** Normal. **Artillery** *Hostile*: very active on duckboard track in morning. *Own*: Active. Relieved by 116 M.G. Coy in the line at 3pm – good relief – no casualties. **Aircraft** Both active.	1/

Army Form C. 2118.

13

WAR DIARY
or
INTELLIGENCE SUMMARY.
(Erase heading not required.)

Instructions regarding War Diaries and Intelligence Summaries are contained in F. S. Regs., Part II. and the Staff Manual respectively. Title pages will be prepared in manuscript.

Place	Date	Hour	Summary of Events and Information	Remarks and references to Appendices
CARNARVON CAMP (M10 B4.3)	25th		Parades : 9.15 am to 3pm. Inspection. Cleaning guns and repacking limber & checking stores. Foot inspection etc.	
			Weather	
	26th		Parades. Normal training carried out	
			Xth Corps Routine Order No 292	Immediate Awards
			Military Medals	
			66653 L/cpl C.T. Dewitt, 86347 Pte E.J. Pendrick, 45099 Sgt A. Dunster, 53762 Sgt J.M. Ganguhason	
			Weather Heavy rain all night and morning	

D. D. & L., London, E.C.
(A8041) W1 W7771/M2931 750,000 5/17 Sch. 82 Forms/C2118/14

Army Form C. 2118.

WAR DIARY
or
INTELLIGENCE SUMMARY.
(Erase heading not required.)

Place	Date	Hour	Summary of Events and Information	Remarks and references to Appendices
CARNARVON CAMP.	27.		Parades. Route March. RENINGHELST - WESTOUTRE - CANADA CORNER & CAMP. Weather. Bright sunny day but cold	
	28.		C of E Church Parade at RENINGHELST 9am. 39th Div Order No 199. "39th Div will relieve 4th Div in the line on the night of 28/29." 118th Bde in line – 117th Reserve. Machine Gun Relief to be carried out on 29th & night of 29/30th. O C Coy to Bn HQ to arrange re relief. See Operation Order Appendix 3.	
TOWER HAMLETS SECTOR	29.	am 5.30	8 guns of 228 M.G. Coy relieve 4 guns of 220 M.G. Coy near CLONMEL COPSE ("D" Battery Position) 8 guns to remain in Divisional Reserve 8 guns of 117 M.G. Coy relieve 4 guns of 22 M.G. Coy at "B" Battery (J 25 c 6.3) & occupy "A" Battery positions (4 guns) at J 25 b 4.9 (Re 16 guns of "A" & "B" "D" Battery to be under the command of O.C 228 M.G. Coy for tactical purposes. Move 2 Motor lorries conveyed 8 gun teams of 228 Coy from CARNARVON CAMP to SHRAPNEL CORNER	
		am 4.30	Arrived VERBRANDEN MOLEN ROAD (I 28 a 8.5) ZILLEBEKE 28 NW 4 & NE 3	

Army Form C. 2118.

WAR DIARY
or
INTELLIGENCE SUMMARY.
(Erase heading not required.)

Instructions regarding War Diaries and Intelligence Summaries are contained in F. S. Regs., Part II. and the Staff Manual respectively. Title pages will be prepared in manuscript.

Place	Date	Hour	Summary of Events and Information	Remarks and references to Appendices
TOWER HAMLETS SECTOR	29th		Relief complete 10.30 a.m. Situation - Quiet up to 10 a.m. Coy. HQ taken over at HEDGE STREET TUNNELS. A.B.D. Batteries are employed for barrage work, chiefly on S.O.S. The S.O.S. Lines allotted to each Battery are as follows.	15

Battery	Location	No. of Guns	S.O.S. Lines		Mean Range
"D"	T.25.a.3.8	6	T.27.c.45.45 – T.27.b.15.30		2,300 x
"A"	—	2	T.27.b.15.30 – T.27.b.50.90		2,500 x
"B"	T.25.a.65	4	T.27.b.50.90 – T.22.c.05.15		2,600 x
"A"	T.25.b.3.8	4	T.22.c.05.15 – T.22.c.60.45		2,500 x
"G"	T.19.d.6.5	6	T.22.c.60.45 – T.22.d.18.98		2,900 x

{238 Coy, 117 Coy, 118}

Move of Camp. CARNARVON CAMP. (M5c.1.8) evacuated by 11 a.m. & Reserve Gun Teams Transport & Rear HQ moved to CHEAP CAMP. (M15 & 49) approx. Sheet 28 SW 1/20,000.

Army Form C. 2118.

WAR DIARY
or
INTELLIGENCE SUMMARY.
(Erase heading not required.)

Instructions regarding War Diaries and Intelligence Summaries are contained in F.S. Regs., Part II. and the Staff Manual respectively. Title pages will be prepared in manuscript.

Place	Date	Hour	Summary of Events and Information	Remarks and references to Appendices
TOWER HAMLETS Sector	29.		Hostile shelling fairly heavy in vicinity of Battery Positions 1-3 pm. also later in evening. The usual amount round entrance to HEDGE STREET TUNNELS & Quarries intermittently throughout night	16
	30.		3rd. Div Order No 180. - Second Army to resume attack on S.(a) day. X Corps to simulate attack on GHELUVELT & BECELAERE 118th Inf Bde to put up smoke barrage on Div front. M.G.s to cooperate with Artillery.	
		ZERO HOUR 6.50	All guns of 'A' 'B' 'D' Batteries fired in accordance with Div Instruction (G.G.1/14) from 5.50 to 6.30am on selected areas	
			Battery Targets Area Rds	
			A. (2guns) 1 J.34.a.34 3,250	
			A. (1gun) 2 T.28.a.58 1,250	
			A. (1gun) 3 T.22.c.10 1,000	
			B. (2guns) 1 T.28.c.19 3,000	
			8,500	
			Batt Target Area Rounds	
			B. (1gun) 2 T.28.a.04 1,950	
			B. " 3 T.29.a.48 1,500	23,450
			A. (6guns) 1 J.336.45 8,750	
			D. (2 ") 2 T.29.c.95 3,250	
			15,250 } 23,450	
			8,500 }	
			9 O.Rs wounded	See 14

Army Form C. 2118.

WAR DIARY
or
INTELLIGENCE SUMMARY.
(Erase heading not required.)

Instructions regarding War Diaries and Intelligence Summaries are contained in F. S. Regs., Part II. and the Staff Manual respectively. Title pages will be prepared in manuscript.

Place	Date	Hour	Summary of Events and Information	Remarks and references to Appendices
TOWER HAMLETS sector	30th		Retaliation in reply to our Barrage only slight, at first behind our front line system, lifting 35mins later to Batteries in rear. Rest of day moderately quiet, but own Artillery active.	
			Weather very cold – ground drying until 1 pm when rain until 3.p.m	
			M.G. Harassing fire at irregular interval 6pm 30th to 6 am 31st	
			Targets engaged Tracks about J.22.c.11 3000 rds } Returned Dug Outs at J.27.c.86 3000 } Total Tracks at J.27.c.44 3000 } 9,000	9000
	31st		Situation unusually quiet morning fairly heavy miscellaneous shelling in p.m. Large quantity of Gas Shells put over all round HEDGE ST TUNNELS between 5-7 pm; the nearest shelling of checkerboard traces etc throughout night	Strength of Coy O OR 10 + 159 See A
			Weather Fair – much warmer – Bgt S.W wind. M.G. Harassing fire as usual 6.30pm to 6 am. Returned Total 9000.	9000

Appendix No 1

Operation Orders.
by Capt J. A Royds
Com. 228 M. G. Coy.

Refce maps
France 28 S.W.
ZILLEBEKE 28 NW + NE.

14/10/17

In accordance with 39 Div Order 145. of 13th. 39th Div will relieve 37 Div in TOWER HAMLETS Sector on night of 15/16 Oct.
Barrage Machine guns will be relieved by 8 guns of 228 M G Coy + 8 guns of 117 Bde MGC Remaining 8 guns of 228 Coy will remain in Div Reserve at transport lines N 9 d central

Transport — 1 Limber with 8 guns and equipment + 4 belt boxes per gun to be at I 28 a 9 5 junction of TOWSEYS TRACK and VERBRANDEN ROAD at 2.45 pm on 16.

Guides — from 111 M. G. Coy will meet gun teams at I 28 a 9 5 at 3 pm. Tripods and 10 belt Boxes per gun will be taken over

Teams — will consist of 4 men per gun 1 Officer + 2 NCO per section. Each section will provide two guns from the line with 1st Aid + SP box complete.

Coy HQ — will be at HEDGE STREET TUNNELS. CSM + 2 signallers will report at Coy HQ with phones etc before guns are relieved.

Runners — 2 runners Radford + Lease will be detailed to remain at Coy HQ and 1 with each section

Relief Complete — to be reported by runner to Coy HQ and list of trench stores taken over handed in.

Information — all possible information to be obtained at gun position + all calculations etc taken over

Trench feet — Section officers will see that every man in their section has two pairs of serviceable socks before proceeding to trenches + all precautions against trench feet will be taken
Socks will be changed daily, feet washed

and rubbed with whale oil. Officers will personally superintend this

Move — No 1 + 2 Sections + HQ party detailed above will be prepared to proceed to the line by Motor lorries, leaving vicinity of billets at 12.30 pm on 16th. Debuss at I 32 a 9.4
Remainder of Coy in reserve will march to new transport lines at N9 d central
Dinners for all will be at 11.30 am.
Move off at 12.30 pm

Advance Party G.S wagon with baggage will move off at 10 am with a guide to arrive at N9 d central before 1.30 pm.
Two signallers with bicycles will accompany the G.S Wagon.
One Sergt and 8 men will accompany the lorry conveying stores and blankets moving off at 12.30 pm. They will make all possible preparations in the new camp. The coy arrive and have tea ready by 4 pm.

Officers Valises To be packed and ready to be placed on G.S. wagon at 9.15 am

Limber for the line will move off at 9 am.
Any officers pack etc to go up the line to be packed on limber by 8.30 am.
Men will carry packs with great coats

Appendix No 2

Operation Orders
by
Capt J A Royds.
Comdg 228 M G Coy   23/10/17

1.   8 guns of 228 M G Coy & 8 guns of 118 M G Coy will be relieved by 16 guns of 116 M G Coy during the day of 24th inst.

2. Guides   1 guide per battery & 1 for HQ will meet incoming teams near CANADA TUNNELS at 2pm. Each guide will have a slip giving his Battery letter & no of incoming section he is to meet.

        "A" Battery No 2 Section Lt Pritchard
        "B"   "   No 4 Section Lt. Crosser
        "D"   "   No 1 & 3   "   Lt. Hale

3. Limbers   2 half limbers one for mens packs, one for gun equipment will approach as near as situation permits to CANADA TUNNELS 3.15 pm.

Telephone equipment should if possible be carried on limbers.

4. Taking Over   8 Tripods & 14 belt boxes per gun will be handed over. Receipts will be obtained for all stores handed over including S.A.A (in bulk) traps etc etc

5. Relief Complete to be reported personally by S officers to Coy HQ at the TUNNELS and wired through in Code to 39 Div HQ

6. Change of Camp   on relief Coy will proceed to CARNARVON CAMP M10b99 on road from RENINGHELST to CANADA Corner. Any party detached from main party will be given a written chit with name & map reference of new camp.

7. Guides   2) will meet outcoming teams at the BRASSERIE 5pm & conduct them to M10b99
The senior N.C.O. present will collect all outcoming gun teams at the BRASSERIE & ensure that there are no stragglers before moving off.

Officers chargers   If possible will be at BRICK STACK at 4pm

Appendix No 3.
28/10/17

Operation Orders
by Capt. J. A. Royds.
Comdg 228 M. G. Coy.

1. In accordance with 39th D.O. No. 179.
    a) 8 guns of 228 M G Coy will relieve 4 guns of 220 M G Coy at D' battery positions on 29th inst.
    b) 8 guns of 119 M G Coy will take over A battery position (J 25 b 4 y) at present unoccupied and B battery position (J.25 a 6 3) relieving 4 guns of 22 M G Coy.
    c) All guns mentioned in (a) & (b) will be tactically under the command of O.C 228 M G Coy.

2. Relief (a) 2 guides for B battery will meet incoming teams of 119 M G Coy at JUNCTION of TOWSEYS TRACK at the VERBRANDEN road at 7.30 am on the 29th
    b) 119 M G Coy will provide their own guides for A Battery
    c) No guides will be required for D battery

3. a) Stores, equipment etc. No exchange of tripods & belt boxes will be made at positions.
    b) All available belt boxes and spare belts to be at positions by night of 29th.
    c) List of stores including S.A.A. taken over to be submitted to Coy HQ (228 Coy) at HEDGE ST TUNNELS by 12 noon 29th.

4. Transport O/C Coy will make their own arrangements for carrying guns & equipment to the line.

5. Relief Complete to be reported to Coy HQ at TUNNEL at earliest possible moment.

6. a) Communication will be by wire from each battery to HQ at TUNNELS.
    119 M G Coy will take in at least 2 telephones which must be in good working order and 2 signallers who will be responsible for maintenance of the line to A & B batteries from the test box. 228 M G Coy will require 3 telephones & 2 signallers who will ensure that communication is kept up from HQ to test box & then to D battery
    b) Runners will be required in addition at rate of 1 per section of 4 guns at Battery positions, also 1 runner per battery at Coy HQ.

7. Accomodation being limited gun teams will be cut down to the minimum.

P.T.O.

8. Trench Feet. All standing orders with regard to care of feet will be strictly adhered to and officers will be held personally responsible for any neglect in this direction.

9. Situation, casualty, firing report etc. will be rendered daily before 8am to Coy HQ at TUNNELS

10. All instructions, information, maps, calculation etc will be taken over by relieving officers. Instruction with regard to S O S barrage lines etc will be issued later.

11. Conveyance of Personnel. Buses will be at CONFUSION CORNER and CARNARVON CAMP at 6am. & 5.30am respectively for 11 y & 228 n. S. Coy. & parties will debuss at SHRAPNEL CORNER

12. Acknowledge

To 3a Division

Herewith War Diary for
November 1917, please.

C. P. Aldridge
Capt.,
for O. Comdg. No. 228 Machine Gun Coy.

War Diary
for
1st November 1914 - 30th November 1914.
Volume 5.

WAR DIARY
or
INTELLIGENCE SUMMARY.
(Erase heading not required.)

Army Form C. 2118.

Vol 5

Place	Date 1917	Hour	Summary of Events and Information	Remarks and references to Appendices
TOWER HAMLETS Sector Refce map ZILLEBEKE 1/10,000 28 NW 4 & NE.3	Nov 1st		228 M.G Coy. allotted Road "D" Battery position (J.25.a.36) with 8 guns for Barrage purpose + Harrassing fire by night. O.C 228 Coy Res also 8 guns of 114 M.G Coy under his command for tactical purpose – "D" Battery 4 guns at J.25.b.38. "B" at J.25.a.6.5. 4 guns M.G Harrassing fire Targets Tracks about J.24.a.29 } Rounds fired & MARGATE FARM } 5450 1.30pm 15/6 and Nov 1st Searching Track J.21.C.2.1. to H.1. 3.000	8450
			Situation Abnormally quiet morning – Heavy Miscellaneous Shelling of the naval area started about 12.30pm + continued through afternoon. Gas Shells on Track J.35.a.4.5 + round HEDGE ST. TUNNELS 6 - 6.30pm repeated 10.30pm + distributed pretty freely at night. Enemy M.Gs putting indirect fire over on Track J.25.a.4.8 Own M.Gs Harrassing fire on tracks at J.24.b.4.4 3000 rds Tracks + Dugouts at J.24.a.9.b 5,000.	Strength 8000. O. ors 9 150 Horses + mules 51
			Weather Heavy mist early. Fine day. Mild S.E wind.	

Army Form C. 2118.

WAR DIARY
or
INTELLIGENCE SUMMARY.
(Erase heading not required.)

Instructions regarding War Diaries and Intelligence Summaries are contained in F.S. Regs., Part II. and the Staff Manual respectively. Title pages will be prepared in manuscript.

Place	Date	Hour	Summary of Events and Information	Remarks and references to Appendices
TOWER HAMLETS Sector Map ZILLEBEKE or SHREWSBURY FOREST 1/10,000	2nd		Weather - Mostly & damp all day. Mild N.W. wind. Less activity in all direction. Duck heard Kacks Shells intermittently all night & gas Shells appeared to be going over to back area. Enemy Arty - Slightly active round tracks by night. Own M.G. Harassing fire. Tracks at J.22.C.2.1. 3250 Rds 6.30 p.m. - 6 a.m. Tracks fork of MARGATE F.M. 5250.	8,500 Reinforcements both Coys in from kits
	3rd		12,000 Rds S.A.A. carried up to No 9 battery positions Bam. Situation as usual. Artillery Active at dawn quietening down until near Ratten more active during afternoon. No gas shells noticed. Enemy M.G. fire as usual at night. Enemy aircraft noticed flying low over our lines at 11 am 2 P.M. 4.30 & 6.15 p.m. engaged by rifle & M.G. fire without success. Owing to the mist impossible to follow the flights of own machines. Own M.G. Harrassing as usual - Tracks at J.24.b.44. 2,500 rds (6.30 p.m. to 6 a.m.) - Tracks dump outs J.24c.96. 6,000 Rds. Weather fair - Wind 12 M.P.H. S.E.	8,500 Reinforcements O. ORs 9. 101 Stores Trunks 51

Army Form C. 2118.

WAR DIARY
or
INTELLIGENCE SUMMARY.
(Erase heading not required.)

Instructions regarding War Diaries and Intelligence Summaries are contained in F. S. Regs., Part II. and the Staff Manual respectively. Title pages will be prepared in manuscript.

Place	Date	Hour	Summary of Events and Information	Remarks and references to Appendices
TOWER HAMLETS Sector	4th		Reliefs during the night of 3rd/4th. 116th Inf Bde relieved 118th Bde in the Line. Inter-section reliefs only in M.G. Barrage batteries A B D (228 & 119 m.g Coy) remain	
			Situation a quiet morning. Further reliefs safely carried out – also 30,000 rounds S.A.A. carried up to m.g positions	
			Heavy shelling of entrances to HEDGE ST TUNNELS 2pm onwards	
			Hostile Artillery more active all day than usual after gun Rell at LEWIS HOUSE	
			M.Gs active at night apparently from direction of night	
			a J.29.b.06.	
			own M.G. Harassing as usual Targets Tracks at J29.b.44 3000 rds	9000
			6pm to 6am	J29.c.96 6000
				Aug 6 wks
			Aerial Activity only slight	
			Weather Mild & fine	
				Strength OR. a x
				51

Army Form C. 2118.

WAR DIARY
or
INTELLIGENCE SUMMARY
(Erase heading not required.)

Instructions regarding War Diaries and Intelligence Summaries are contained in F.S. Regs., Part II. and the Staff Manual respectively. Title pages will be prepared in manuscript.

Place	Date	Hour	Summary of Events and Information	Remarks and references to Appendices
TOWER HAMLET Sector	5th		39th Div. Order No.184 In conjunction with operations further North 51st Div. is attacking POLDERHOEK CHATEAU. R.M.G.C. to issue instructions whereby M.G's cooperate with Barrage fire on GHELUVELT area & also by M.G. fire on selected targets. Decided to put forward the 8 guns of 'D' Battery, 228th M.G. Coy. a matter of 900x in order to be within effective range for Indirect Barrage fire on GHELUVELT. A.M.G.O. + O.C. 228 reconnoitred & selected suitable position for battery near EVE FARM (J26 A 15) Part of gun equipment moved up by day & guns load before dusk in new positions - Fortunately a particularly quiet day with track most early only clearing about 10am. Enemy M.G. Active as usual by night Own M.G. Active Harassing as usual. - J24.6.44 4000rds	OKKered 4000 Strength 9 Off 156 OR Horses Mules 51

Army Form C. 2118.

WAR DIARY
or
INTELLIGENCE SUMMARY
(Erase heading not required.)

Instructions regarding War Diaries and Intelligence Summaries are contained in F.S. Regs., Part II. and the Staff Manual respectively. Title pages will be prepared in manuscript.

Place	Date	Hour	Summary of Events and Information	Remarks and references to Appendices
TOWER HAMLETS Sector	1st		Zero Hour fixed for 6.0am MGs of A B D Batteries fired as below from 6.30am to 6.45am	6
			A Batt. 2 guns Target T28a.5.b & 8.8 - 3,000 rds Road cutting	
			6.3am " " T28a.6.0 1,490 Junction of Roads	
			6.17am " " T28.C.18 1,560 DUPLEX FARM	
			B Batt. " " T.24a.39 1,500 MARGATE FARM	
			6.3 " " T.24.C.95 1,450 Group of Dugouts	
			6.17am " " T33b.29 3,000 ALASKA HOUSES	
			D Batt. 8 " Area W of T22d central 21,000 GHELUVELT	
			6.3 to 6.45am Total Rounds 33,000	33000
			Artillery. Doubtle. Replied to our barrage but gradually quietened down	
			Enemy Aircraft noticed flying very low over our positions several times during day. Engaged by rifle & M.G. fire without success (500 rds)	500
			Enemy M.G. Naval activity from 8am	
			Own M.G. Harassing fire - Target about T.24.B.40.30 - 2 guns - 6,300 rds	9000
			" T.22.C.2.1 - 1 - 3,000 rds	Stoppages 0 + 8enbo 51

WAR DIARY
or
INTELLIGENCE SUMMARY.
(Erase heading not required.)

Army Form C. 2118.
6

Place	Date	Hour	Summary of Events and Information	Remarks and references to Appendices
TOWER HAMLETS Section	6th		Gas:- Several of the men at Kansport Lines (returned from line on 4th) complain of sore throat & chests. Apparently delayed action though little gas was smelt during tour & respirators worn when it was detected.	6
	7th		General Situation:- A fairly quiet morning. Hostile artillery activity during afternoon afterwards normal.	
			Hostile M. Gs.- Usual harassing of Kreek at night.	
			Own M. Gs. Harassing at night targets - J.24.B.54 - 2500 rds. J.24.B.44 - 2000 rds. J.27.B.29 - 2000 rds. J.21.d.92 - J.27.b.44 - 6000 rds.	12,500 Ads
			Hostile Aircraft Active especially during night when several bombs were dropped on our lines. Several low flying machines engaged with AA guns - no results - 500 rds fired	500
			Own Aircraft Active	Strong R — OR Q 135/160 Nozora Amber 51

Army Form C. 2118.

WAR DIARY
or
INTELLIGENCE SUMMARY.
(Erase heading not required.)

Instructions regarding War Diaries and Intelligence Summaries are contained in F. S. Regs., Part II. and the Staff Manual respectively. Title pages will be prepared in manuscript.

Place	Date	Hour	Summary of Events and Information	Remarks and references to Appendices
TOWER HAMLETS Sector	8th		Relief: In accordance with 39th D.O. 186 the 8 guns of 114 M.G. Coy were relieved by 116th M.G. Coy in A & B Batteries	
			General Situation: A quiet day with some artillery counter battery work	
			Hostile Aircraft: Very active but at good heights — 100 rounds fired	100
			Own — Very active	
			Hostile M.G. — Usual Harassing on tracks during the night	
			Own — Harassing fire at night Targets T24 b.6500 — 1450 T29 C.9.6 — 1450 T29 b.3.4 — 3000	6,500
	9th		General Situation — Artillery more active than yesterday otherwise normal	
			Hostile Artillery — Very active shelling roads & tracks, day & night	
			Own — " — Very active	
			Hostile M.G. — Quieter	
			Own M.G. — Harassing fire at night Targets T24 b.6500 — 1450 T29 C.90.60 — 4000 T29 C.90.65 — 3500 T29 b.45.25 — 2000 T29 b. 35.40 — 1500 ——— 12450	Strength O - officers 9 + 156 Horses/Mules 51 12,450

Army Form C. 2118.

WAR DIARY
or
INTELLIGENCE SUMMARY.
(Erase heading not required.)

Instructions regarding War Diaries and Intelligence Summaries are contained in F. S. Regs., Part II. and the Staff Manual respectively. Title pages will be prepared in manuscript.

Place	Date	Hour	Summary of Events and Information	Remarks and references to Appendices
TOWER HAMLET Sector	9th		Aircraft very active Weather dull - rain during night	Reinforcements 1480 Evacuation 2080 (0)
	10th		General Situation normal Artillery (a) Hostile - active during day on tracks etc quiet all night (b) Own - active In Go. (a) Hostile - active on tracks all night (b) Own - Harrassing fire all night 6 pm - 6 am Targets J27 & 45.30 8000 rds J27 & 45.25 3000. Aircraft below normal Weather rain 3rd Aus Cmn 169 (a) The 39 Div will extend its left to cro REUTEL BEEK relieving 5th Div on night 11/12 Nov. (b) The 3g Aus will hold front now held will be transported to IX Corps at 10 am 12 Nov. (a) On receipt instructs Place on the night 10/11 Nov. + 11 Nov. (c) 226 Inf. Bn G Coy. will provide barrage battery of 8 guns under instructions to be issued Lup D.M.G.O.	6000 Strength O. 720 O.R. 1472 Horses Mules 51

Army Form C. 2118.

WAR DIARY
or
INTELLIGENCE SUMMARY.
(Erase heading not required.)

Place	Date	Hour	Summary of Events and Information	Remarks and references to Appendices
MENIN ROAD Sector Ref. Map. GHELUVELT 1/10,000 Sheet 28 NE3	11th		Move. D Battery evacuated + we occupied the dug-in in accordance with A.O.169 + relieve 205 in C Coy (see Appendix No 1). Relief. No. 1+2 Sections take over new positions with 8 guns a 3rd Section move to Transport lines at CHEAP CAMP and to be in Divl Reserve. SOS lines left when POLDERHOEK CHATEAU at {J22 c9 y (POLDER HOEK Spur)} to {J14 c08} G Relieve - J21 c22 to C95 to J22 c11 (CHELUVELT SPUR) Right about J14 c6.5 to J24 b68 to 40 (TOWER HAMLET SPUR) Relief Spandau opened normal on Relief Spandau fire intensified & covered the Right flank & saluting of our ground. Relief. Have completed quite uneventful quite uneventfully about 4am. General Situation Normal. Artillery (a) Hostile intermittent activity (b) Own active	Strength O OR O + 15½ NonCom- batants 5½
	12th		Weather fine with occasional showers. General Situation Normal Artillery (a) Hostile quiet during day active during night (b) Own normal	

Army Form C. 2118.

WAR DIARY
or
INTELLIGENCE SUMMARY.
(Erase heading not required.)

Instructions regarding War Diaries and Intelligence Summaries are contained in F.S. Regs., Part II. and the Staff Manual respectively. Title pages will be prepared in manuscript.

Place	Date	Hour	Summary of Events and Information	Remarks and references to Appendices
MENIN ROAD Sector	12		Aircraft - Nil (a) Hostile Harassing at night duck board tracks etc (b) Own Normal Weather fine	Strength O 86 10 445 Horses/Mules 51
	13		General Situation morning quiet but normal rest of day Artillery (a) Hostile quiet in morning but active towards evening night. Shelling our right of battery position at 5.30pm. Hr. J.E. Battelemy (reinforcement) (b) Own Normal S.O.S answered on extreme left 11.30 pm Aircraft below normal In Gen Normal Weather fine misty General situation normal	
	14		Artillery (a) Hostile quiet until 8 pm then heavy shelling during night (b) Own Normal	

Army Form C. 2118.

WAR DIARY
or
INTELLIGENCE SUMMARY.
(Erase heading not required.)

Instructions regarding War Diaries and Intelligence Summaries are contained in F. S. Regs., Part II. and the Staff Manual respectively. Title pages will be prepared in manuscript.

Place	Date	Hour	Summary of Events and Information	Remarks and references to Appendices
MENIN ROAD SECTOR	14		M.G.o. (a) Rifle usual harassing (b) Guns 4 guns fired on the left S.O.S line to disperse a reported enemy concentration. 1.55pm - 2.30pm rds fired 2000 Aircraft below normal Weather fine	2,000
	15		General situation unchanged Artillery (a) Hostile - One Rm intense shelling 5am-6am Rifles fairly active through day & night (b) Own normal M.G.o (a) Hostile as usual (b) Own 2 guns fired alternately behind normal S.O.S lines from 11.50pm to 5.45am 16/11/19 rds fired 4000 Aircraft below normal Weather fine	4,000

Army Form C. 2118.

WAR DIARY
or
INTELLIGENCE SUMMARY.
(Erase heading not required.)

Instructions regarding War Diaries and Intelligence Summaries are contained in F.S. Regs., Part II. and the Staff Manual respectively. Title pages will be prepared in manuscript.

Place	Date	Hour	Summary of Events and Information	Remarks and references to Appendices
MENIN ROAD Sector	16		General situation unchanged	
			Artillery (a) Ours: Quieter than usual at dawn & throughout morning. Were shelling from 12.30 p.m. to 6 p.m. Seeing gun crews on battery areas a few falling men down position	Rendezvous 10R
			(B) Own: Normal	Cavalation 11CRa
			M.G.s (a) Hostile: Very active throughout day & night. Harassing	
			(a) Own: Normal	
			(b) Hostile: NIL	
			(b) Own: Below normal	
			Aircraft:	
			Weather: Fine - misty	
			None:	Strength
			In accordance with Brue instructions the transport lines & personnel including 'A' Section in Rosun move from CHEAP CAMP, and proted by 2 p.m. Good camp recently occupied by R.E.'s	O 0 OR 162 Horses + Mules 51

D. D. & L., London, E.C.
(A8021) Wt. W1771/M2031 750,000 5/17 Sch 52 Forms/C2118/14

100

Army Form C. 2118.

WAR DIARY
or
INTELLIGENCE SUMMARY
(Erase heading not required.)

Instructions regarding War Diaries and Intelligence Summaries are contained in F. S. Regs., Part II. and the Staff Manual respectively. Title pages will be prepared in manuscript.

Place	Date	Hour	Summary of Events and Information	Remarks and references to Appendices
MENIN Road Sector	17		Relief. Intersection relief within the Company. (Emma Barrage Battery Position) B/L Section relieved 1/2 Section who proceed to RIDGEWOOD.	
			General Situation quiet & misty. Large quantity of mustard gas reported to be hanging about nr. battery area from last night. Shelling. Relief completed 2.30am. no casualties.	
			Artillery Hostile quiet during morning. But very active at intervals during afternoon. Mostly on checkboard trench near our battery positions. Own Normal	
			M.G. Hostile Harassing a little by day. More at night. Own as usual.	
			Weather very misty.	N.C.O. to U.K. Course of Instruction. 1 O.R. wounded.
18			General Situation quieter than usual throughout day. Hostile Artillery & M.Gs. intermittent shelling throughout trenks at night.	Strength 10 M55162 Horseshoes 51
			Weather fine dry. Visibility good. Aircraft normal.	C.P.A.

Army Form C. 2118.

WAR DIARY
or
INTELLIGENCE SUMMARY.
(Erase heading not required.)

Place	Date	Hour	Summary of Events and Information	Remarks and references to Appendices
MENIN RD Sector	19		General Situation quiet except for shelling & MG fire on Railway. One of the battery guns & an extra gun mounted in the vicinity of STIRLING CASTLE at dusk to do harassing fire. Targets tracks at J.7.y.b. & J.22.a.w.D. Also 4000	4000
	20		Weather fine & dry, visibility good. General Situation normal. Artillery active all day, trench batteries & Guns active. MG o Routine Harassing fire on tracks & around battery HQ at night. Guns Harassing fire 6pm to 2am to cover Targets J.28.a.8. 2000, Tracks J.22.c.D. 2000, night Aircraft both very active after midday until dusk. Weather bright sunny fine.	4000 Strength O 6 O/R 10 +439 162 Horses Mules 51

WAR DIARY or INTELLIGENCE SUMMARY

Army Form C. 2118.
15

(Erase heading not required.)

Place	Date	Hour	Summary of Events and Information	Remarks and references to Appendices
MENIN ROAD Sector	2nd		General Situation normal	
			Artillery (a) Hostile normal intermittent shelling of tracks etc during day. Battery active around battery OPs from 6.45pm to 7.30pm, after normal	
			(b) Own normal	
			M.Gs (a) Hostile normal harassing fire day & night	
			(b) Own 2 gun positions made at T14 & 29.30 from which they harassed 10 pm to 6.30 am 29/11/17 Target tracks behind S.O.S. line 4000 yds	4000
			2 guns harassed from vicinity of STIRLING CASTLE on Targets T27 & 3.5 3000 yds T22.C 4000 yds 3000 yds	4000
			1 gun harassed from 2am to 6am on tracks in T16.b 450 yds	450
			All guns were laid on LEFT S.O.S. from 2am until dawn as enemy attack was expected from that direction as its cutter	Strength OR 10 Horses mules 51

Army Form C. 2118.

WAR DIARY
or
INTELLIGENCE SUMMARY.
(Erase heading not required.)

Place	Date	Hour	Summary of Events and Information	Remarks and references to Appendices
MENIN Road Sector	22		General Situation Normal quieter than usual	
			Artillery below normal	
			M.G's (a) Hostile never harassing day & night	
			(b) Own 6 guns cooperated with gas attack on GHELUVELT at 6.15pm Target normal S.O.S. lines to cover 800 yds 4000	4000
			" " 3000	3000
			2 guns harassed from J.14 b 29 30 to 3000 yds	4000
			2 " " from vicinity of STIRLING CASTLE 4000	
			Target tracks at J.14.c. J.14.b & J.2.c	
			Aircraft active	
			Weather fine in morning, dull & wet	
	23		Relief No 3&4 Sections relieved by 1/2 Section in some battery positions	
			No 3H.H. - to RIDGE WOOD road relief	
			Completed 8.30am Casualties nil	
			Artillery (a) hostile quiet during day, but active on duckboards night	Strength
			normal	O Officers 10 ORs
			(b) Own	Horses/Mules 51

WAR DIARY
or
INTELLIGENCE SUMMARY.
(Erase heading not required.)

Army Form C. 2118.

Place	Date	Hour	Summary of Events and Information	Remarks and references to Appendices
MENIN ROAD SECTOR	23		Aircraft (a) Hostile Harassing as usual	
			(b) Own Harassing at night from 5pm to 6:30am	
			2 guns at J.14.b.29.30 - Targets - J.25.b.14 - 2000 rds	
			J.23.a.54 - 2000 rds	8000
			2 guns at J.19.b.40.50 - Targets - J.24.c.60.35 - 2000.	
			J.22.d.10.20 - 2000.	
			Weather Normal Fair	
			Artillery (a) Hostile Quiet during morning but active in afternoon and during night	Reinforcements 4 ORs
			(b) Own Normal	Evacuations 1 Offr
			Aircraft Below normal	
	24		M.G.s (a) Hostile - Usual Harassing	
			(b) Own - Harassing from 5pm to 6:30am	
			2 guns at J.14 & 29.30 Targets J.22.c.03.65 } 4000	8000
			J.22.b.64 }	Strength
			2 - J.19.b 40.80 - J.24.55.40 } 4000	O 10 ORs
			J.28.a.10.95 } 80.00 Rds	Horses/mules 51
			Weather Fair - Right wind	

Army Form C. 2118.

WAR DIARY
or
INTELLIGENCE SUMMARY.
(Erase heading not required.)

Instructions regarding War Diaries and Intelligence Summaries are contained in F.S. Regs., Part II. and the Staff Manual respectively. Title pages will be prepared in manuscript.

18

Place	Date	Hour	Summary of Events and Information	Remarks and references to Appendices
MENIN ROAD Sector	25.		General Situation quieter than usual	
			Artillery (a) Hostile much quieter than previous day intermittent shelling during night	Ammunition 50R's
			(b) Own below normal	
			Aircraft Nil	
			M.G's (a) Hostile quieter than usual	
			(b) Own Harassing at night 5.30 pm to 6 am	
			2 guns J.14 & 29.30 Targets J.23.a 6.4 } 4000 rds	
			J.19.c 40.35 } 4000 rds	8000
			2 guns J.19.c 40.80 – J.24.6 55.40 } 4000 rds	
			T.28.a 10.45 } 4000 rds	8000
			Weather fair Regt wind	
	26th		39 Div O1 195 28/11/17	
			(1) The 39 Div (Less Artillery) will be relieved by 30th Div & transferred to VIII Corps by 10 a.m. 29/11/17	
			(2) (c) Machine Guns, T.M Bty reliefs will be carried out in the right section on the night 25/26 Nov & in the left section on the night 26/27 Nov.	Strength O Offs 0 OR 10 165 158 Horses/Mules 51
			The D.M.G.O. will issued the necessary instructions for the relief at 228 Inf. Coy.	

Army Form C. 2118.

WAR DIARY
or
INTELLIGENCE SUMMARY.
(Erase heading not required.)

Instructions regarding War Diaries and Intelligence Summaries are contained in F.S. Regs., Part II. and the Staff Manual respectively. Title pages will be prepared in manuscript.

19

Place	Date	Hour	Summary of Events and Information	Remarks and references to Appendices
MENIN ROAD SECTOR to RIDGE WOOD	26		5(a) G.w.clef the 39 Div will carry out training in STEENVOORDE AREA. Relief. The 226 m G Coy relieved our 8 guns in the battery position at 19 gun 226 m G Coy with 19 gun 89 m G Coy relieved 2 guns at T19.c.40.50 at 4.30 p.m. (see appendix 2) The teams relieved proceeded to camp at RIDGE WOOD. General situation unchanged.	Casualties O.R.s wounded
CAESTRE Ref Map Belgium & Pt of France Sheet 27; 1/40,000	27		Move. The company left RIDGE WOOD at 9.15 a.m. & marched to GODEWAERSVELDE thence by route march to billets near CAESTRE, arriving at 2 p.m. entrained at 11.30 a.m. to OUDERDOM. The transport did not commence its journey until midday owing to difficulty in getting lorries through dry around RIDGE WOOD. Route: RENINGHELST, GODEWAERSVELDE, EECKE & breeto arriving 6 p.m. Officers, HQ, 2 Section, Transport, billeted at farm Rennes Q.8.b.2.4. 1 Section billeted in front for Rome Lines & Lantern. Accommodation: good. (see appendix No 3) 2 Section billeted at farm Rennes P.30.d.6.6 accommodation good both faring are on main road from CAESTRE to CASSEL	Strength O.R.s 10,151 Horses/Mules 51

Army Form C. 2118.

WAR DIARY
or
INTELLIGENCE SUMMARY.
(Erase heading not required.)

Instructions regarding War Diaries and Intelligence Summaries are contained in F. S. Regs., Part II. and the Staff Manual respectively. Title pages will be prepared in manuscript.

Place	Date	Hour	Summary of Events and Information	Remarks and references to Appendices
CAESTRE Ref map Belgium Prov France Sheet No 27 1/40000	27	Weather	Heavy rain morning clearing in afternoon	
	28	Parades.	9.15am Inspection, 9-30am - 12.30pm Cleaning Guns / gun equipment Limbers etc & clothing	
		Weather	fine	
	29	Parades	9.15am - 12.30am Inspection, P.T., cleaning guns, remainder of Limbers	
		Weather	fine	
	30	Parades	8.45am - 12.30pm Training carried out as usual. (Bath in afternoon) 11 ORs (reinforcements)	Strength O 0 10 102 Horses/Mules 51
		Weather	Dull wet at intervals	

Appendix I
10/1/17.

Operation Orders
by
Lieut R.W. Fyffe
Acting O.C. 228 M.G. Coy.

Evacuation.

The 8 gun teams at present occupying D Battery will evacuate that position on the morning of the 11th inst. and return to Cheap Camp.
4 half limbers will be at Canada St. Tunnels at 7.0 A.M. on the morning of the 11th to convey guns & gun equipment back to camp.

Relief.

228 M.G. Coy less 8 guns will relieve 4 guns of 205 M.G. Coy at Barrage Positions J.14.d.4.9 on the morning of the 11th inst.
The 8 gun teams will consist of
No 1 Section under 2/Lt Whitehead
" 2   "   "   "   " Hawkins

Guides.

From Coy Hdqrs of 205 M.G. Coy in Ridgewood will meet the limbers at the Brasserie at 4.30 A.M. on the 11th inst & guide them up to the ration dump.
Four guides from the battery position will meet the teams at 7.0 A.M. at the ration dump & guide them up to the position

4 tripods & 32 belt boxes will be taken over from 205 Coy and receipt given for same, on presentation of this receipt at rear Hdqrs. 6ft at Camp M.15.c.65.75. 2/Lt Yule will hand over the no. specified to 205 Coy & obtain receipt for same.

Equipment

8 guns, 4 tripods, 48 belt boxes, Clinometers etc. will be brought in by the incoming team.

SOS line

fired on at present by the 205 Coy guns, will be our SOS line for 4 guns until new targets are allotted.

Personnel

with guns { 2 Officers
           { 4 men per team
           { 2 NCOs per section

Headquarters

O.C. & batman
C.S.M.
6 Signallers
2 Runners.

Battery Hdqrs   Fitzclarence Farm
Coy   "   J.19.b.3.9.

Runners

The Hdqrs runners with Company their team, will on their look out as they return at the 2nd Coy Hdqrs

Rations will be delivered at the ration
dump at 3:30 AM every morning.
Water can be obtained at points at
J 14 c 25.30

Operation Orders
by
Lieut R W Fyffe
Actg O.C. 226 M.G. Coy.

Relief Orders

226 M.G. Coy will relieve 228 M.G. Coy in the Polderhoek Section on the evening of the 26th. 5 guns of the 226 Coy will relieve 5 guns of 228 Coy at "D" Battery. 5 tripods & hot fête boxes will be handed over to 226 Coy & receipts obtained for same.
1 gun of 226 Coy will relieve 1 gun of 228 Coy at the position at Coy Hdqrs.
1 gun of 89 M.G. Coy will relieve 1 gun of 228 Coy at the position at Coy Hdqrs. on the evening of the 26th.

Guides

for team of 89 M.G. Coy will be at junction of E Track & Plumers Drive at 4.30 P.M. prompt 26th.
for 5 teams of 226 M.G. Coy relieving guns at "D" Battery will meet the 226 Coy teams at ration dump at 4.0 P.M. on the 26th. Mr Thorburn will see that these men are detailed from men at the battery.

2 guns & 2 tripods with spare parts (& like bore, over & above the 6 to be handed over (at Dv Batt.) will be sent back to Transport lines on ration limber on morning of 26th. O.C. Dv Batt. will be responsible that this gun equipment is down at the ration dump in time. If the ration limber is unable to get up to the dump, the two guides who go to meet it will inform the T.O. that gun equipment is to go back & limber must wait until it is loaded.

Limbers

Two half limbers will be up at the ration dump at 5.45 P.M. prompt on evening of 26th. The senior Section Sgt. in the line will be at the ration dump & will check everything as it is put on the limbers & he will not allow the limbers to move off until everything has been loaded, (including gum boots) high gum boots will not be handed over.

Trench Stores

A receipt must be obtained for all handed over.

On relief sections will proceed to Ridgewood under N.C.O.s to be detailed

O.C. "D" Battery will report "Relief complete" to Bay Hdqrs.

Appendix VII
Operation Orders
by
2/Lt J Yule
for OC 228th Coy

The Company will move to-morrow
to Billets near Caestre
All blankets will be rolled up in
bundles of 20 by 7.0AM Sections
will transfer their own blankets
over to the lorry dump
Full marching order will be worn
and haversack rations carried.
Breakfast will be at 7.0AM
A/Cpl Farrington will report to
Coy Orderly Room at 7.30 from to
Lorry Park. The following will
    constitute the above.
  2/Lt Aldridge
  L/Cpl NS.
  Pte Donnelly
  8 men (to be detailed by Orderly Sgt)
The 8 men will relieve the guard
over the lorry dump at 7.30 A.M.
and will load lorries when they
arrive at 8.15 A.M.
  2/Lt Aldridge will report to the
Orderly Officer before moving off.
Officer's valises to be packed by
8.0 AM and will be taken over

to the dump. The Orderly Sgt will
detail 10 men to help Officers
servants to carry valises etc.
remainder of Company will clean
up the camp.
Orderly Officer will inspect camp
at 8.30 AM.
Section Sgts will draw haversack
rations from the QM Stores at 7.30 AM
The Officer's Mess cook and Pte Holland
will proceed to billets with the
Motor Lorries and will have a meal
ready when the Coy arrive.
Transport will move off at 8.30 AM
under order of the TO

Guides Cpl Green with Transport
        L/Cpl Cameron " Motor Lorries
        Pte MacMillan " Coy

War Diary

December 1917

228 Coy.
Machine Gun Corps.

R W M He Lieut.
for Comdg. No. 228 Machine Gun Coy.

Army Form C. 2118.

WAR DIARY
or
INTELLIGENCE SUMMARY.
(Erase heading not required.)

Instructions regarding War Diaries and Intelligence Summaries are contained in F. S. Regs., Part II. and the Staff Manual respectively. Title pages will be prepared in manuscript.

Place	Date	Hour	Summary of Events and Information	Remarks and references to Appendices
Between CAESTRE & ST. SYLVESTRE CAPPEL	Feb 1		Parades Route March :- Billets to CAESTRE - EECKE - GODEWAERSVELDE - EECKE - Billets	Reinforcements 1 O.R. O.Rs 162
			Weather Fine	
Refer M/ch				
HAZEBROUCK 5ᴬ 1/40,000	2		Parades C.O's inspection - C of E. Church Parade in Billets	Evacuations 2 O.Rs (sick)
			Weather Fine	
	3		Parades 8.30 A.M. to 12.30 P.M. Inspection - P.T. - Pack-saddlery drill & action from limbers - Gun drill - Care & cleaning	
			2.0 P.M. to 4.0 P.M. Recreation	
			Weather Fine	
	4		Parades 8.30 A.M. to 12.30 P.M. Usual (Box respirators inspected & adjusted by Div.l Gas Officer)	
			2.0 P.M. to 4.0 P.M. Recreation	
			Weather Cold & Frosty	

Army Form C. 2118.

WAR DIARY
or
INTELLIGENCE SUMMARY.
(Erase heading not required.)

Instructions regarding War Diaries and Intelligence Summaries are contained in F. S. Regs., Part II. and the Staff Manual respectively. Title pages will be prepared in manuscript.

Place	Date	Hour	Summary of Events and Information	Remarks and references to Appendices
	5		Parades 8.30A.M. to 12.30P.M. Inspection - Road March	
			2.0 P.M. to 4.0 P.M. Recreation	
			Weather cold	Reinforcement
	6		Parades 8.30A.M. to 12.30P.M. As usual	15 O.Rs.
			2.0 P.M. to 4.0 P.M. Recreation	
			39th Division Order 199	
			2. The 39th Division (less Artillery) will proceed to the LUMBRES area and will on arrival come under orders of the X Corps.	
			3(a) For the move 228 M.T. Coy will be grouped with 118th Infantry Brigade Group.	
			(b) Personnel will move by train - 118th Infantry Brigade Group from GOEWAERSVELDE to NIELLES on 8th inst.	
			(c) Transport will move by route march - 118th Infantry Brigade Group on 7th inst. to RENESCURE and on 8th inst. to LUMBRES (see Appendix)	

WAR DIARY
or
INTELLIGENCE SUMMARY.

(Erase heading not required.)

Army Form C. 2118.

Place	Date	Hour	Summary of Events and Information	Remarks and references to Appendices
Picardies	7		Usual	
			Move The transport will proceed to LUMBRES area under the 118th Brigade Transport Officer.	
			March route To RENESCURE via CASSEL on 7th inst. RENESCURE to LUMBRES area via ARQUES & WIZERNES on 8th inst.	
			After Order 39th Divisional Order 199	
			(b) 228 M.G. Coy on arrival at NIELLES-LEZ-BLEQUIN will proceed by route march to VAL-DE-LUMBRES where they will remain. Billets from area commandant LUMBRES	
			118th Inf Brigade Order 165	
			2(a) The Brigade Group (less 228 M.G. Coy) will entrain at GODENAERSVELDE and detrain at NIELLES-LEZ-BLEQUIN. The 228 M.G. Coy will entrain at CAESTRE (otherwise as 39th Divisional Order 199) 2nd 12.40 P.M. Appx.	

WAR DIARY
or
INTELLIGENCE SUMMARY.
(Erase heading not required.)

Army Form C. 2118.

Place	Date	Hour	Summary of Events and Information	Remarks and references to Appendices
VAL DE LUMBRES	8		Move. In accordance with 39th Divisional Order 199 & 118th Infantry Brigade Order 165, the company left billets at mid-day entraining about 2.0.P.M. at CAESTRE, detraining at LUMBRES about 6.0.P.M. and marched to billets at VAL DE LUMBRES - 2 miles.	O.Rs. 10 O.Rs. 176
Ref:- Map 1/100,000	9		During this period the Company carried out intensive training every morning for 4 hours, and recreational training every afternoon. Divisional competitions in football, cross country running & Tug-of-war were successfully carried out, the company showing great keenness.	Reinforcements 10th 1 O.R. 12th 1 " 13th 1 " 14th 1 " Evacuated 2 O.Rs (Sick)
HAZEBROUCK S.A. 28	6		39th Divisional Order 203 1. The 39th Division (less Artillery) will move from the LUMBRES area, and will relieve the 32nd Division in the Right Division Sector II Corps Front on 29th, 30th & 31st December 1917. 2. Personnel will move by train and transport by road to march.	

WAR DIARY
or
INTELLIGENCE SUMMARY.
(Erase heading not required.)

Army Form C. 2118.

Place	Date	Hour	Summary of Events and Information	Remarks and references to Appendices
Ref^{ce} Map. HAZEBROUCK 5A 1/100,000 Sheet 28			39th D.O. 203 (conta)	
			4. For the purpose of the move Units will be grouped as in Appendix A. 228 M.G.Coy with 117 Brigade Group.	
			5 Relief of Machine Guns will be carried out on the 31st December and night 31st Dec 1917/1st Jan 1918.	
			(1) 228 M.G.Coy will relieve the 219th M.G.Coy. Details for relief will be arranged between the C.O's concerned. Relieving M.G. Coys will send one Machine Gunner per gun team into the line 24 hours prior to date of relief.	
			Move table to accompany 39th D.O. 203.	

Date	Unit	From	To	Route	Remarks
28/12/17	Transport of 117 Bde Group	LUMBRES Area	ST MONELIN	ST MARTIN AU LAERT	
29/12/17	117 Bde Group	LUMBRES Area	Support Bde Area to relieve 96 Bde	WINNIZEELE – WATOU	Train from WIZERNES
29/12/17	Transport 117 Bde Group	ST MONELIN Area	ST JANETER BIEZEN D. area (228-Boy Border (cmh.)	POPERINGE – SWITCH RD – VLAMERTINGHE	
30/12/17	Transport 117 Bde Group	ST JANETER BIEZEN	Support Area	LINE	
30–31/17	117 Bde	Support Area	LINE		To relieve 14 Bde
31/12/17 – 1/1/18	228 M.G.Coy	Support Area	LINE		To relieve 219 M.G.Coy

WAR DIARY
or
INTELLIGENCE SUMMARY.
(Erase heading not required.)

Army Form C. 2118.

Place	Date	Hour	Summary of Events and Information	Remarks and references to Appendices
			Administrative Instructions in connection with 39th D.O. 203.	
			2. Accommodation	
			(c) The 228 M.G. Coy will be accommodated at IRISH FARM on arrival until 219 M.G. Coy moves out of CANAL BANK. Transport will double up with that of 219 M.G. Coy.	
	28		Move. The Transport will move under orders issued by Officer i/c 117 Bde Group Transport, joining the column at Road Junction 300 yds E of CHATEAU LEONNETTE on LUMBRES - SETQUES ROAD 11.0 A.M. To water & feed ready to join rear of column at 11.30 A.M.	Reinforcements 1 O.R. Evacuate 1 O.R. (Sick)
			Personnel moves on 29th. Train leaving WIZERNES at 7.0 A.M.	
	29		Baggage lorries unable to reach billets overnight owing to check industries, all stores, blankets, etc man-handled to lorries, approximately 2 miles distant between 11.30 & 2.0 A.M.	O O.Rs 10 181

WAR DIARY
or
INTELLIGENCE SUMMARY.
(Erase heading not required.)

Army Form C. 2118.

Place	Date	Hour	Summary of Events and Information	Remarks and references to Appendices
	29		Company marched off from VAL DE LUMBRES 4.0 a.m (clue WIZERNES 6.0 a.m) moving with 117th Brigade group. Column delayed by bad roads and incidents.	
			Train moved off 8.30 a.m.	
			Arrived ST JEAN Station 11.30 a.m. Marched to IRISH FARM Camp; men accommodated in tents, Officers in Nissen Hut.	
	30		Reconnaissance of gun positions by O.C. Coy. with O.C. 219 M.G. Coy 7.0 a.m. to 1.0 p.m. and arrangements made for relief on 31st	Evacuation 1. O.R.
	31		8 guns of 228 M.G. Coy relieved 8 guns of 219 Coy (32nd Div'l M.G. Coy) at YETTA HOUSES d.3.d.6.6. Relief complete 10.30 a.m.	Evacuation 1. O.R.
			4 guns of 228 M.G. Coy relieved 4 guns of 219 Coy in the Corps Line – 2 guns at GENOA d.i.c.7.7, 2 at VON TIRPITZ FARM d.7.b.35.70. Relief complete 10.0 a.m.	1. O.R.b v.k. for course of instruction.

WAR DIARY
or
INTELLIGENCE SUMMARY.
(Erase heading not required.)

Army Form C. 2118.

Place	Date	Hour	Summary of Events and Information	Remarks and references to Appendices
	31		Divisional Defence Scheme of 32nd Division allotted Battery at YETTA Huts S.O.S. Barrage Line V.21.d.15.70. to V.22.d.25.20. also in front of PASSCHENDAELE if required. Harassing fire by day and night.	

From OC

To 39th Division

Herewith War Diary for
January 1918

R.C. Fyffe Lewis
2nd Lieut. Comdg. No. 228 Machine Gun Coy.

127

228 M GC[oy]

WAR DIARY or INTELLIGENCE SUMMARY
Army Form C. 2118.
(Erase heading not required.)

Place	Date	Hour	Summary of Events and Information	Remarks and references to Appendices
ST JULIEN SECTOR	Jun 1st 1918		228 M.G. Coy held "E" Battery position - at YETTA HOUSES D.3.d.6.6. with 8 guns: also 4 guns on bope line of which 2 guns at GENOA ⎱ 2 guns at VON TIRPITZ FARM ⎰ D.1.c.7.2 D.7.b. 35.70.	
Ref Map POELCAPPELLE SPRIET 1/10,000			M.G. Harrassing Fire Carried out by 4 guns at YETTA HOUSES during night 31/5/1/6 Targets V.22.b. 80.12 V.22.b. 25.25 V.22.a. 37.692 V.22.a. 10.20 ⎱ Rounds fired 6,000 ⎰	6,000
			Situation	
			Enemy Artillery active on church tower tracks & YETTA HOUSES between 9.0am & 12. noon 7.&.6 intervals during night, otherwise very quiet.	
			Enemy Aircraft very active all night, no machines observed by day	
			Enemy M.G.'s Nil	
			Weather fine & frosty	

WAR DIARY
or
INTELLIGENCE SUMMARY.
(Erase heading not required.)

Army Form C. 2118.

Place	Date	Hour	Summary of Events and Information	Remarks and references to Appendices
ST JULIEN SECTOR	Jan 2		Weather Still very cold, snow in the evening	Transferred 3 OR's
			Enemy Artillery Again active on duck board tracks around YETTA HOUSES between 10.0 a.m. & 3.0 p.m.	
			ALBATROSS FARM heavily shelled between 2.45 p.m. & 3.45 p.m.	
			Enemy Aircraft Fairly active all the morning at a great height, none came within range of Anti Aircraft MGs	
			Our Artillery Active all day	
			Our M.G.s Harassing fire. Targets V.22.a.2.4 V.21.b.45.10 V.21.b.05.20 V.23.d.3.5 } Rounds fired 6,000	6,000
	Jan 3		Enemy Artillery Intermittent shelling all day, mostly shrapnel intensified at dusk & continued for an hour, mostly directed on tracks & a greater proportion of H.E. used. Shelling continued till midnight. Gas shells dropped around YETTA HOUSES at 11.30 p.m.	
			Our Artillery not very active	
			Enemy Aircraft active during morning, none came within range of our "A.A." MGs.	

WAR DIARY
or
INTELLIGENCE SUMMARY.
(Erase heading not required.)

Army Form C. 2118.

Instructions regarding War Diaries and Intelligence Summaries are contained in F. S. Regs., Part II. and the Staff Manual respectively. Title pages will be prepared in manuscript.

Place	Date	Hour	Summary of Events and Information	Remarks and references to Appendices
ST JULIEN SECTOR	Jan 2		Own M.G. harassing fire Targets V.22.b.80.12 / V.22.b.25.25 / V.22.a.9.5 / V.22.a.10.20 } Rounds fired 6,750	6,750
	cont'd			
	Jan 3		2 guns of 118 M.G. Coy relieved 2 guns of 228 M.G. Coy at GENOA D.1.c.7.2.	
			2 guns " " " " VON TIRPITZ FARM D.7.b.35.70	
			Relief complete by 9.30 am.	
			No 2 section of 228 M.G. Coy relieved No 3 section of 228 M.G. Coy at YETTA HOUSES	
			Relief complete by 9.30 am. Casualties NIL	
			Nine coy Hdqtrs removed from IRISH FARM to CANAL BANK. men in reserve were accommodated in bivvies. Officers in 1 dugout.	
			Accommodation very poor.	
	Jan 4		Situation	Attached
			Enemy Artillery much less active than in previous day	12 O.R.
			Own Artillery quiet	
			Aircraft very few machines observed	
			Own M.G. harassing fire Targets V.22.a.3.3 / V.21.b.5.2 / V.21.b.0.3 / V.23.d.5.4 } Rounds fired 5,750	5,750

WAR DIARY
or
INTELLIGENCE SUMMARY.
(Erase heading not required.)

Army Form C. 2118.

Place	Date	Hour	Summary of Events and Information	Remarks and references to Appendices
ST. JULIEN SECTOR	Jan 4		12 men of 116 Infantry Brigade attached to 228 M.G. Coy	
	Jan 5		Situation	Extreme Cons
			Enemy Artillery very quiet, more active during night bursts of shrapnel periodically	2 Ors
			Battn line position: 20,000 rounds of S.A.A. taken up to Corps line and placed at positions as follows:	Tour for Coy 1 OR
			STROPPE FARM 10,000 rounds	
			CLIFTON HOUSE 10,000 rounds	Strength
			Decided to keep No 3 Section permanently on fatigue on Corps line position	Officers Ors 10 175 attached 12
			Harassing fire Targets V.22.a.2.4. V.22.b.45.10 V.21.b.05.20 V.23.d.3.5 } Rounds fired 6,250	
			Own M.G.	6,250
	Jan 6		Relief No.1 Section relieved No.2 Section at YETTA HOUSES relief completed by 9.30 am casualties Nil.	

Army Form C. 2118.

WAR DIARY
or
INTELLIGENCE SUMMARY.
(Erase heading not required.)

Instructions regarding War Diaries and Intelligence Summaries are contained in F. S. Regs., Part II. and the Staff Manual respectively. Title pages will be prepared in manuscript.

Place	Date	Hour	Summary of Events and Information	Remarks and references to Appendices
ST JULIEN SECTOR	Jan 6		Situation	
			Enemy Artillery normal, periodic shelling of tracks round battery area, mostly shrapnel	
			Our Artillery fairly quiet except for occasional hurricane bursts.	
			Enemy Aircraft a number observed none within range, one enemy machine brought down by one of our planes at 2.30 pm	
			Our Aircraft very active at low altitude	
			Our M.G. Harassing fire Targets V.22.b.25.25 V.22.a.85.25 V.22.a.6.2 V.22.a.2.4 } Rounds fired 6,450	6,450
			1 Officer returned from Infantry course	attached
			12 men attached from 118 Infantry Brigade making in all up to date 23.	11 ORs
	Jan 7		Situation	
			Enemy Artillery normal, periodic shelling of tracks mostly shrapnel	
			Own Artillery very quiet except for occasional bursts.	

Army Form C. 2118.

WAR DIARY
or
INTELLIGENCE SUMMARY.
(Erase heading not required.)

Instructions regarding War Diaries and Intelligence Summaries are contained in F. S. Regs., Part II. and the Staff Manual respectively. Title pages will be prepared in manuscript.

Place	Date	Hour	Summary of Events and Information	Remarks and references to Appendices
ST JULIEN SECTOR	Jan 7		Enemy Aircraft NIL	
			Own Aircraft NIL	
			Weather Rough, snow & rain in evening	
			Cotoline 20,000 rounds SAA taken up to Cotoline & dumped as follows No 3 Aviation 10,000	
			No 4 — 10,000	
			Own M.G. Harassing fire Targets V.22. C. 9.5 / V.22. d. 2.4 / V.22. b. 9.12 / V.22. b. 25.25 Rounds fired 6,500	6,500
	Jan 8		Situation	
			Enemy Artillery very active all day. YETTA HOUSES & vicinity shelled by 7.7m gun from 12.30 pm to 1.30 pm & again at 4 - 5 pm. Quiet during night	
			Enemy Aircraft very active all day, flying very high	
			Own Artillery active during day, quiet during night	
			Enemy M.G. more active than on previous days.	

WAR DIARY or INTELLIGENCE SUMMARY

Army Form C. 2118.

Place	Date	Hour	Summary of Events and Information	Remarks and references to Appendices
ST. JULIEN SECTOR	Jan 8		Our M/G Harassing fire Targets V.22.a.25.75 – 98.17 V.22.a.6.20 V.22.a.2.4 V.21.b.45.10 } Rounds fired 6,500	6,500
			12 men attacked from 117 Infantry Brigade making total attached men 35.	Attached 12 O.Rs
			Rota line 40,000 rounds S.A.A. carted up to both line positions & dumped as follows:— CLIFTON HOUSE 10,000	
			STROPPE FARM 10,000	
			No 3 position 10,000	
			No 4 " 10,000	
	Jan 9		Relief No 4 section relieved No 1 section at YETTA HOUSES relief complete by 9.30 a.m. Casualties 1 O.R. wounded	
			Situation	
			Enemy Artillery fairly quiet until 1.0 p.m., shelled back all batteries with 77 mm 9 & 2 guns fairly active during night	
			Our Artillery Very active all day	

WAR DIARY
or
INTELLIGENCE SUMMARY.

(Erase heading not required.)

Army Form C. 2118.

Place	Date	Hour	Summary of Events and Information	Remarks and references to Appendices
ST. JULIEN SECTOR	Jan 9		Enemy Aircraft. Fairly active. Not arther range of "DO" M.E.	
			Own Aircraft. Very active	
			Own M.Gs. Harassing fire Targets V.21.b.45.10	
			V.21.b.05.2 } Bursts fired	
			V.23.d.3.5	
			V.22.d.4.75	5,750
	Jan 10		Coy. line 20,000 rounds SAA carried up to YETTA HOUSES by working party of 40 men handed from KANSAS X ROADS	5,750
			Situation	
			Enemy Artillery Normal	
			Own Artillery Normal	
			Own M.Gs. Harassing fire Targets V.22.b.25.25	
			V.22.a.25.75 } Bursts fired	
			V.22.a.6.2	
			V.23.a.2.4	7,500
			1 Officer relieved from Coy. to BORDEAUX	7,500
	Jan 11		Situation	
			Enemy Artillery active during morning, put down a barrage on our front from 1.30 p.m. to 2.45 p.m. quietened down afterwards & quiet all evening.	

Army Form C. 2118.

WAR DIARY
or
INTELLIGENCE SUMMARY.
(Erase heading not required.)

Rnr

Place	Date	Hour	Summary of Events and Information	Remarks and references to Appendices
ST JULIEN SECTOR	Jun 11		Our Artillery very active during morning replied to enemy barrage. Quiet remainder of day.	
			Aircraft of both sides very few observed	
			Enemy M.G. Harassing fire Target V.22.c. 9.5 V.22.d.2.4 V.22.b.25.25 } Rounds fired 6,000	6,000
			1 Officer & 16 ORs reinforced personnel at YETTA HOUSES Officer in charge of both Line M.G. emplacements eighteen 8gun emplacements at No1 2" 19" CLIFTON HOUSE D7.b.75.2 5" STIROPPE FARM D.1.c. 95.00 6" 9" 10" D.I.C. 35.45 11" 4" 12" D.I.C. 25.55	
			20 men employed constructing offen emplacements at these co-ordinates.	
			Material taken up to YETTA HOUSES for construction of dug outs for extra personnel	

WAR DIARY
or
INTELLIGENCE SUMMARY.
(Erase heading not required.)

Army Form C. 2118.

Place	Date	Hour	Summary of Events and Information	Remarks and references to Appendices
ST JULIEN SECTOR	Jan 12		Relief No.2 Section relieved No.4 Section at YETTA HOUSES. Relief complete by 10.0 am	
			Situation	
			Enemy Artillery fairly active throughout the day. WELLINGTON FARM lightly shelled with 5.9's during afternoon	Evacuated 3 O.Ths
			Our Artillery usual activity shown	
			Enemy Aircraft not much activity shown	
			Our Aircraft fairly active all day	Strength O. 10 O.R. 172 attached 33 6,000
			Our M.G.s Harassing fire Targets V 21.6 45.10 / V 21.6 03.20 / V 23.d 30.50 / V 22.d 40.75 Rounds fired 6,000	
	Jan 13		Enemy Artillery very quiet all day, just occasional bursts of shrapnel over tracks	
			Our Artillery very quiet	
			Enemy Aircraft active all day, none came within range of "AA" M.G.s	
			Our Aircraft fairly active	

Army Form C. 2118.

WAR DIARY
or
INTELLIGENCE SUMMARY.
(Erase heading not required.)

PWR

Instructions regarding War Diaries and Intelligence Summaries are contained in F. S. Regs., Part II. and the Staff Manual respectively. Title pages will be prepared in manuscript.

Place	Date	Hour	Summary of Events and Information	Remarks and references to Appendices
ST JULIEN SECTOR	Jan 13		Enemy M.G's NIL	
			Own M.G's Harassing fire Target V.22.c.9.5 V.22.d.2.4 V.22.b.8.12 V.22.b.25.25 } Rounds fired 5,500	5,500
	Jan 14		Enemy Artillery fairly active throughout period special attention being paid to all tracks KRONZ PRINZ shelled with 5.9's during the afternoon.	
			Enemy Aircraft none observed	
			Enemy M.G's only slight activity shown	
			Our Artillery quiet all day & night	
			Our Aircraft none observed	
			Our M.G's Harassing fire Targets V.22.a.20.40 V.21.b.45.10 V.21.b.15.20 V.23.d.30.50 } Rounds fired 6,000	
	Jan 15		No 1 section relieved No 2 section at YETTA HOUSES, relief complete by 9.30 am } carried to gun position by No 1 section 80,000 rds S.A.A. 30 "A" Trench frames 50 sheet corrugated iron	

Army Form C. 2118.

WAR DIARY
or
INTELLIGENCE SUMMARY.
(Erase heading not required.)

Place	Date	Hour	Summary of Events and Information	Remarks and references to Appendices
ST. JULIEN SECTOR	Jan 15		Enemy Artillery Active on back areas	
			Enemy Aircraft Nil	
			Enemy M.G. Fairly quiet	
			Own Artillery Active all day	
			Own Aircraft Nil	
			Own M.G. Harassing fire. Targets V.22.d.40.75 V.22.d.9.5 V.22.d.2.4 V.22.b.20.12 } Rounds fired 5,750	5,750
			Weather rained all night. Trend at YETTA HOUSES water-logged shelters nearly all collapsed.	
	Jan 16		Enemy Artillery active during morning on tracks etc. KRONZ PRINZ shelled all morning. Quiet during afternoon.	
			Enemy Aircraft Nil	
			Enemy M.G. Nil	
			Own Artillery Active throughout period	
			Own Aircraft Nil	

Army Form C. 2118.

WAR DIARY
or
INTELLIGENCE SUMMARY.
(Erase heading not required.)

Place	Date	Hour	Summary of Events and Information	Remarks and references to Appendices
ST. JULIEN SECTOR	Jan 6		Our M.G's harassing fire. Targets V.22.6.25.25 V.22.a.85.25 to 98.17 } Bds fired V.22.a.6.2 V.22.a.2.4	6,000
			Weather rain all day; impossible to keep men at guns. Position more than 2 days, no shelters & trench water-logged	
	Jan 7		New Section relieved No 1 Section at YETTA HOUSES, relief complete by 9.30 am.	
			Enemy Artillery fairly quiet except from 9.0 pm to 10.0 pm when area in rear of battery positions was shelled with 5.9"s	
			Enemy Aircraft slightly active, none came within range of "A.A." M.Gs	
			Enemy M.Gs fairly quiet	
			Our Artillery Third activity shown except for occasional hurricane concentration	
			Our Aircraft not very active	

WAR DIARY
or
INTELLIGENCE SUMMARY.
(Erase heading not required.)

Army Form C. 2118.

Place	Date	Hour	Summary of Events and Information	Remarks and references to Appendices
ST. JULIEN SECTOR	May 17		Our M.G. harassing fire. Targets V.22.d.40.75 V.22.b.90.50 } Rounds fired V.22.d.2.4 } 6,000 V.22.b.80.12	6,000
	18		Enemy Artillery very active during whole period, KRONPRINZ area heavily shelled during the afternoon.	
			Enemy Aircraft much activity shewn, none came within range of "A.A." M.G.	
			Enemy M.G. very active	
			Our Artillery very active all day, especially the Scured quiet during the night	
			Our Aircraft much activity shewn all day	
			Our M.G. harassing fire. Targets V.22.b.25.25 V.22.d.2 V.21.b.45.10 } Rounds fired V.23.d.3.5 } 6,000.	6,000
			Officers at gun positions tested (1) Telescopic Aiming Disc (2) Deflection Bar Foresight } Report quite satisfactory (3) Magie Firing Box	

Army Form C. 2118.

WAR DIARY
or
INTELLIGENCE SUMMARY.
(Erase heading not required.)

Place	Date	Hour	Summary of Events and Information	Remarks and references to Appendices
ST JULIEN SECTOR	Jan 19		No 3 Section relieved No 4 Section at YETTA HOUSES	Evacuated
			relief complete by 9.30 am	5 ORs
			Enemy Artillery very quiet throughout the period	Reinforcements
			Enemy Aircraft none observed	4 ORs
			Enemy M.G. NIL	Strength
			Our Artillery only slight activity shown	Officers 0ths
			Our Aircraft Nil	10 171
			Our M.G. harassing fire Target V.22.d 40.75) Rounds fired	attached 35
			V.22.b 92.50)	
			V.22.d 20.40)	
			V.22.b 80.12) 6,000	6,000
	Jan 20		Enemy Artillery active throughout the period	
			Enemy Aircraft active notes within range of "AA" M.G.	
			Enemy M.G. active	
			Our Artillery very active all day quiet during the night	
			Division being relieved by 35th Division	
			116 Brigade in line relieved night of 20/21st	

Army Form C. 2118.

WAR DIARY
or
INTELLIGENCE SUMMARY.
(Erase heading not required.)

Instructions regarding War Diaries and Intelligence Summaries are contained in F.S. Regs., Part II, and the Staff Manual respectively. Title pages will be prepared in manuscript.

Place	Date	Hour	Summary of Events and Information	Remarks and references to Appendices
ST JULIEN SECTOR			Orders received that 228 M.G. Coy would vacate battery positions at YETTA HOUSES morning of 21st	
			Our M.G. harassing fire Targets { V. 22 a. 20.40 V. 21. b. 45.10 V. 21. b. 15.20 V. 23. d. 30.50 } Rounds fired 6,000	6,000
	21		YETTA HOUSES gun positions vacated at 7.30 am, personnel arrived CANAL BANK 9.30 am Coy entrained at ST JEAN 1.0 pm, arrived BRANDHOEK 2.0 pm, marched to TUNNELLER'S camp. O.R.s billeted in huts, Officers in Nissen huts	
			228 M.G. Coy included in 117 Brigade Group.	
TUNNELLER'S CAMP	22		This day was spent by the Coy in cleaning guns, equipment, clothing etc. & preparing for move secret As on 22nd	
	23			To U.K. for 0/1 OR 1
	24		Received orders that Coy were to entrain the following morning at PROVEN to proceed South to MERICOURT L'ABBE, Coy bathed in afternoon, all preparation for move completed by midnight	

WAR DIARY
or
INTELLIGENCE SUMMARY.
(Erase heading not required.)

Army Form C. 2118.

Place	Date	Hour	Summary of Events and Information	Remarks and references to Appendices
TUNNELLERS CAMP	Jan 25		Coy moved off from TUNNELLERS CAMP at 2.0 am. Horses marched to PROVEN; arrived 3.0 am; entrained with all transport & left PROVEN 4.40 am. Train stopped at TINQUES at 11.0 am for 45 minutes to remove men & animals. 11.45 am left TINQUES and to men, animals, wagons & transport arrived MERICOURT L'ABBE 2.55 pm. Coy & Transport left MERICOURT L'ABBE 3.30 pm & marched to MORCOURT (distance approximately 8½ miles) arrived in billets 8.0 pm. All 4 sections & H/Qrs in School held up en route by Transport of 134 Field Ambulance	Reinforcement 2 Ors S/Lieut H Office P/No 110 '72 attached 35
MORCOURT	26		This day was spent by Coy in settling down in billets CHURCH SERVICE in School at 11.0 am.	
	27		Orders received that Coy would move to line to take over from 21st & 9th Divisional M.G. Coys.	
	28		Parades from 9.0 am to 12.30 am. Afternoon preparing for move to line.	

WAR DIARY
or
INTELLIGENCE SUMMARY.
(Erase heading not required.)

Army Form C. 2118.

Place	Date	Hour	Summary of Events and Information	Remarks and references to Appendices
MORCOURT	Jan 28		Order received 228 Coy attached to 116 Brigade for move	
"	29		Parades from 9.0 am until 12.30 pm	
			Orders received from 116 Bde that Coy would entrain at CORBIE at 6.0 pm 30th inst.	
	Jan 30		Transport left MORCOURT at 7-30 am and proceeded via MARICOURT, SUR SOMME, CHAIGNOLLES, FROISSY, BRAY, SUSANNE, MARICOURT, CLERY to HAUT ALLAINES arriving 6.0 pm	
HAUT ALLAINES			Coy left MORCOURT midday marched to CORBIE arriving 4-0 pm entrained 5-0 pm, train started 6-0 pm. Arrived PERONNE 10-15 pm marched to HAUT ALLAINE, arrived 12-30 am 31st billeted in Tents	
	Jan 31st		Coy left HAUT ALLAINE 8-30 am marched to FINS, arriving 1-0 pm. No 2 & 3 sections relieved 2 sections of 197 M.G. Coy in line relief complete 6-30 pm.	
			No 4 section relieved 1 section of 62 M.G. Coy, complete 7 pm. H.Q, Transport & No 1 section remained at FINS.	

WAR DIARY or INTELLIGENCE SUMMARY.

Army Form C. 2118.

Place	Date	Hour	Summary of Events and Information	Remarks and references to Appendices
GOUZEAUCOURT SECTOR	1918 Feb 1st		Nos 2, 3, & 4 Section in the line	
			Gun position. No 2 Section in the left Brigade Sector attached to 118 M.G. Coy	
			Location Ref. Map. 57 c. S.E. 2	
				Gun No.
			Q. 29. c. 10. 90.	L. 14
			Q. 29. c. 40. 60.	L. 13
			Q. 29. c. 20. 10.	L. 12
			Q. 29. c. 90. 80	L. 11
			No 3 Section in the centre Brigade Sector attached to 116 M.G. Coy	
			Location Ref. Map. 57c. S.E. 4	Gun No.
			W. 6. c. 00. 80	R. 16
			W. 12. a. 50. 70	R. 15
			W. 12. c. 60. 65	R. 14
			W. 12. c. 70. 50	R. 13
			No 4 Section in right Brigade Sector attached to 117 M.G. Coy	
			Location Ref. Map. 57c. S.E. 4	Gun No.
			W. 24. a. 55. 90	L. 18
			W. 24. d. 80. 80	L. 17
			W. 24. d. 80. 75	L. 9
			W. 29. d. 95. 95	L. 15

WAR DIARY
or
INTELLIGENCE SUMMARY.
(Erase heading not required.)

Army Form C. 2118.

Place	Date	Hour	Summary of Events and Information	Remarks and references to Appendices
GOUZEACOURT SECTOR	Feb 1st		No 1 Section in Reserve at FINS carried out training. Special instruction given to attached men.	
			Situation NORMAL	
			Enemy Artillery opened rather heavy fire on our right Brigade at 6.15 am. our own artillery replied & fire died down about 6.50 am.	
	Feb 2nd		Enemy Aircraft slight activity shown, one plane crossed our lines at 9.0 am. flying at about 900 ft. At 2.30 p.m. an E.A. flew over our lines firing into the trenches both were engaged by rifle, Lewis, & M.G. fire	
			Intelligence rather active. attack carried out with Field & heavy guns.	
			M.G. carried out harassing fire	

Army Form C. 2118.

WAR DIARY
or
INTELLIGENCE SUMMARY.
(Erase heading not required.)

Instructions regarding War Diaries and Intelligence Summaries are contained in F. S. Regs., Part II. and the Staff Manual respectively. Title pages will be prepared in manuscript.

Place	Date	Hour	Summary of Events and Information	Remarks and references to Appendices
GOUZEAUCOURT SECTOR	Feb 2nd		Enemy Artillery about normal, slight shelling of VAUCELETTE FARM & GOUZEAUCOURT	Strength O. 10 Ors. 10 174 attached 36
			E.A. NIL	
			Enemy M.G's active at night	
			Intelligence very quiet	
			Our Artillery usual patrolling of front sectors	
			Our Aircraft very quiet, GOUZEAUCOURT shelled with Gas shells from 7.30 pm to 8.0 pm	
			Enemy Artillery	
			E.A. NIL	
	Feb 3rd		No 1 Section relieved No 3 Section in the centre sector, relief complete by 7.0 pm	1 OR. transferred to 148 M.G. Coy

WAR DIARY
or
INTELLIGENCE SUMMARY.
(Erase heading not required.)

Army Form C. 2118.

RWR

Place	Date	Hour	Summary of Events and Information	Remarks and references to Appendices
GOUZEAUCOURT SECTOR	Feb 4th		Intelligence	
			Our Artillery — at 5.30 am SOS went up from front of left Battalion, left Brigade, & artillery replied immediately on to the S.O.S. lines.	
			Our M.G's — Harassing fire carried out day & night.	
			Enemy Artillery — showed considerable activity at intervals during the day against GOUZEAUCOURT.	
			Enemy M.G's — Quiet by day. usual activity shown at night.	
	Feb 5th		Our Artillery — slight activity shown, at about 7.15 pm fired an S.O.S. Reinforcement lines in retaliation for hostile gas shelling.	1 O.R.
			Our M.G's — Harassing fire carried out at night	
			Our Aircraft — usual patrolling of forward areas	
			Enemy Artillery — GOUZEAUCOURT, VAUCELETTE FARM, GAUCHE WOOD all received a little attention at various times during the day.	
			E.A — fairly active. One flew over HEUDECOURT firing M.G. into the village.	

WAR DIARY
or
INTELLIGENCE SUMMARY.
(Erase heading not required.)

Army Form C. 2118.

Place	Date	Hour	Summary of Events and Information	Remarks and references to Appendices
GOUZEAUCOURT SECTOR	Feb 6th		Intelligence Our Artillery active all day; BONNE LIEU was shelled intermittently from 12 noon to 4.0 pm. Our M.G's usual harassing fire carried out. Enemy Artillery spasmodic shelling during early part of day more active than usual on VAUCELETTE FARM at 5.0 pm. GOUZEAUCOURT was shelled with Gas shells. Enemy M.G's very little activity shown, except against our Aircraft during the day. No 3 Section relieved No 4 Section in the left Brigade sector. Relief complete 7.0 pm.	Reinforcements 2 ORs
	Feb 7th		Our Artillery very quiet all day. S.O.S lines tested. Our M.G's usual harassing fire carried out. Our Aircraft Patrolling as usual Enemy Artillery very quiet Enemy M.G's active at night E.A NIL	

WAR DIARY
or
INTELLIGENCE SUMMARY.
(Erase heading not required.)

Army Form C. 2118.

Instructions regarding War Diaries and Intelligence Summaries are contained in F.S. Regs., Part II. and the Staff Manual respectively. Title pages will be prepared in manuscript.

Place	Date	Hour	Summary of Events and Information	Remarks and references to Appendices
GOUZEAUCOURT SECTOR	Feb. 8th		Intelligence slight activity shown	
			Our Artillery usual harassing fire VILLERS-GUISLAIN being paid special attention to	
			Our M.G's active	
			Our Aircraft active	
			Enemy Artillery 11.15 am to 12 noon GAUCHE WOOD was shelled with 4.2 how'rzs. REVALON FARM, HEUDECOURT & GOUZEAUCOURT shelled with single rounds at intervals during the day	
	Feb 9th		Our Artillery slight activity shown, BONNELIEU shelled intermittently throughout the day.	Strength O. Ors. 10 O.R. 176 Attached 36
			Our M.G's usual harassing fire	
			Our Aircraft usual patrols	
			Enemy Artillery more active than usual on back areas with large calibre shells; VAUCELETTE FARM & GOUZEAUCOURT received the usual attention.	
			Enemy M.G's usual activity at night	
			E.A. slight activity shown	

Army Form C. 2118.

WAR DIARY
or
INTELLIGENCE SUMMARY.
(Erase heading not required.)

Place	Date	Hour	Summary of Events and Information	Remarks and references to Appendices
GOUZEAUCOURT SECTOR	Feb 9th		No 4 Section relieved No 2 Section in the left Brigade Sector. Relief complete by 7.0 pm	
	Feb 10th		**Intelligence** *Own Artillery* general registration carried out *Own M.G's* usual harassing fire *Own Aircraft* usual patrolling *Enemy Artillery* showed increased activity, GOUZEAUCOURT & vicinity being the principal targets from 12.0 to 12.30 and around DEAD MANS CORNER was heavily shelled CHAPEL HILL & VAUCELETTE FARM received the usual attention *Enemy M.G's* active at night *Enemy Aircraft* none observed. Section in reserve ordered to be ready to move to division or either flank or to any sector or division front.	

WAR DIARY
or
INTELLIGENCE SUMMARY.
(Erase heading not required).

Army Form C. 2118.

Instructions regarding War Diaries and Intelligence Summaries are contained in F. S. Regs., Part II. and the Staff Manual respectively. Title pages will be prepared in manuscript.

Place	Date	Hour	Summary of Events and Information	Remarks and references to Appendices
BOUZENCOURT SECTOR	Feb. 11th		Intelligence	
			Our Artillery active all day	
			Our M.G's usual harassing fire	
			Our Aircraft active all day	
			Enemy Artillery slightly active. BOUZENCOURT, GAUCHEWOOD receiving attention	Evac to 1 Officer
			Enemy M.G's usual harassing at night	
			E.A. slight activity shown	
			Attacked men found on the miniature range, all round the lorry	
	Feb 12th		No 2 Section. Transport & H.Q. paraded for bath. at FINS	
			Our Artillery fairly active all day	
			Our M.G's usual harassing fire carried out at night	
			Our Aircraft active all day	
			Enemy Artillery showed a very marked decrease during the day. a few heavy shells fired on back areas.	
			Enemy M.G's usual harassing fire at night	
			E.A. very little activity.	

WAR DIARY
or
INTELLIGENCE SUMMARY.

Army Form C. 2118.

Place	Date	Hour	Summary of Events and Information	Remarks and references to Appendices
GOUZEAUCOURT SECTOR	Feb 12th		No 2 Section relieved No 1 Section in the Centre Brigade Sector. Relief complete by 7.0 pm	
	Feb 13th		**Intelligence**	
			Our Artillery Fairly quiet, carried out some registration between 1.0 pm & 2.0 pm	
			Our M.G's Usual harassing fire by day & night	
			Our Aircraft Usual patrols	
			Enemy Artillery Only slight activity shown; back areas received slight attention, activity increased during the night. CHAPEL CROSSING, HEUDECOURT, & RAILROAD were shelled slightly; a few gas shells fell in GOUZEAUCOURT about 8.0 pm.	
			Enemy M.G's Active at night against GAUCHE WOOD, CHAPEL HILL etc.	
			E.A. Few machines flying high, out of range of AA machine guns	

Army Form C. 2118.

WAR DIARY
or
INTELLIGENCE SUMMARY.
(Erase heading not required.)

Place	Date	Hour	Summary of Events and Information	Remarks and references to Appendices
GOUZEAUCOURT SECTOR	Feb. 14th		Intelligence. Very quiet visibility very bad	
			Our Artillery Carried out harassing fire at night on enemy	
			Our M.G's approaches & new trenches	
			Our Aircraft Nil owing to visibility	
			Enemy Artillery showed little activity during the day, but more active towards night. BOUZEAUCOURT was heavily shelled from 7.0 pm to 9.0 pm	
			Enemy M.G's very active during night, firing over our forward area	
			E.A. Nil	
	Feb. 15th		Our Artillery fairly active throughout the period	
			Our M.G's Carried out the usual harassing fire at night	
			Our Aircraft fairly active	
			Enemy Artillery slight activity shown. Vicinity of QUEENS CROSS shelled with 5.9's from 11.0 to 12.0 noon	

Army Form C. 2118.

WAR DIARY
or
INTELLIGENCE SUMMARY.
(Erase heading not required.)

Instructions regarding War Diaries and Intelligence Summaries are contained in F.S. Regs., Part II. and the Staff Manual respectively. Title pages will be prepared in manuscript.

Place	Date	Hour	Summary of Events and Information	Remarks and references to Appendices
GOUZEAUCOURT SECTOR	Feb 15th		Enemy M.G's active at night, on our approaches	Strength O. 1018
			E.A. fairly active	9 176
			No 1 Section relieved No 3 Section in the right Brigade sector relief completed by 7.0 p.m.	attached 36
	Feb 18th		Our Artillery fairly active all day; in the evening GONNELIEU was shelled fairly heavily	
			Our M.G's usual harassing fire at night	
			Our Aircraft active flying at various altitudes to instruct troops at what altitude Rifle, Lewis & M.G. fire is effective against aircraft	
			Enemy Artillery very quiet	
			Enemy M.G. active at night	
			E.A active especially at night when battery areas trenches & billets were bombed continuously from 6.45 p.m. to 10.0 p.m. FINS, HEUDECOURT & SOREL receiving special attention	

Army Form C. 2118.

WAR DIARY
or
INTELLIGENCE SUMMARY.
(Erase heading not required.)

Instructions regarding War Diaries and Intelligence Summaries are contained in F. S. Regs., Part II. and the Staff Manual respectively. Title pages will be prepared in manuscript.

Place	Date	Hour	Summary of Events and Information	Remarks and references to Appendices
GOUZEAUCOURT SECTOR	Feb 16			
			General Orders received that 4 guns of 228 M.G. Coy in left Brigade sector would be relieved by 4 guns of 191 M.G. Coy on night of 17.2.18 & that the 4 guns relieved would relieve 4 guns of 118 M.G. Coy same night. New position for 4 guns 228 M.G. Coy reconnoitred during morning.	Reconnaissance 1 O.R.
	Feb 17		Own Artillery fairly active throughout period, working parties on N of GONNELIEU engaged during morning	
			Own M.G. usual harassing fire carried out at night	
			Own Aircraft active throughout period	
			Enemy Artillery very quiet	
			Enemy M.G. active during night	
			E.A. fairly active during day; very active during night on back areas.	

WAR DIARY or INTELLIGENCE SUMMARY

Place	Date	Hour	Summary of Events and Information	Remarks and references to Appendices
GOUZEAUCOURT SECTOR	Feb. 17th		4 guns of 197 M.G. Coy relieved 4 guns of 228 M.G. Coy on left Brigade sector, relief complete 6.45 pm. 4 guns of 228 M.G. Coy relieved 4 guns of 118 M.G. Coy on left Brigade sector, relief complete 8.0 pm. Gun position Ref. Map 57c S.E.2. Q.36.a.15.20. Gun No. Q.36.a.20.60. L3 Q.30.c.40.30. L4 Q.30.b.40.35. L7 L8 Orders received from Division that 228 M.G. Coy' H.Q. would move from FINS to camp at Ref. Map. 57c S.E.3. W.7.b.50.70. on 18.2.18.	
	Feb. 18th		Our Artillery fairly active, working parties engaged all along front. Visibility very good. Our M.G. working parties engaged, several harassing fire at night Our Aircraft very active all day	

WAR DIARY
or
INTELLIGENCE SUMMARY.
(Erase heading not required.)

Army Form C. 2118.

Place	Date	Hour	Summary of Events and Information	Remarks and references to Appendices
GOUZEAUCOURT SECTOR	Feb. 18th		Enemy Artillery very quiet, occasional single shot on back areas.	
			Enemy M.G's active on tracks at night	
			E.A. slight activity shown	Reinforcement 1 Officer
			228 M.G. Coy. H.Q. & Transport moved from FINS to camp at W.7.b.50.70. Move complete by 12 noon. Accommodation poor	
			No.3 section relieved No.4 section in the Left Brigade sector, relief complete by 7.0 pm	
	Feb 19th		Our Artillery quiet, visibility poor	
			Our M.G's usual harassing fire at night	
			Our Aircraft fairly active	
			Enemy Artillery very quiet	
			Enemy M.G's active during night	
			E.A. less active than usual	

Army Form C. 2118.

WAR DIARY
or
INTELLIGENCE SUMMARY.
(Erase heading not required.)

Instructions regarding War Diaries and Intelligence Summaries are contained in F.S. Regs., Part II. and the Staff Manual respectively. Title pages will be prepared in manuscript.

Place	Date	Hour	Summary of Events and Information	Remarks and references to Appendices
BOUZEAUCOURT SECTOR	Feb. 20th		**Intelligence**	
			Our Artillery at 4.50 am S.O.S. went up in the Rifle Brigade, artillery opened in response, registration carried out during the day.	
			Our M.G's usual harassing fire at night. S.O.S. line fired on in conjunction with artillery.	
			Our Aircraft fairly active during the day.	
			Enemy Artillery at 4.45 am a heavy barrage was put down on our Right Brigade front line, ceased about 5.20 am. Quiet during day.	
			Enemy M.G's little activity shown during night.	
			E.A. inactive	

WAR DIARY
or
INTELLIGENCE SUMMARY.

(Erase heading not required.)

Army Form C. 2118.

Place	Date	Hour	Summary of Events and Information	Remarks and references to Appendices
GOUZEAUCOURT SECTOR	Feb. 21st		*Intelligence*	
			Our Artillery Fairly active, at 5:40 am for about 15 mins totalling was heavy from the Hyde Brigade	Reinforcing 2 C.R.s
			Our M.G's Harassing fire at night on tracks, E.A's were also engaged during the day	
			Our Aircraft usual activity displayed	
			Enemy Artillery fairly quiet	
			Enemy M.G's very little activity shown during the night	
			E.A. very active	
			No 4 section relieved No 2 section in the Border Brigade S. to	
			Relief complete 7.0 pm	
	Feb 22nd		*Our Artillery* little activity shown	
			Our M.G's usual harassing fire at night	
			Our Aircraft very little activity shown, wea ther bad	

WAR DIARY
or
INTELLIGENCE SUMMARY.
(Erase heading not required.)

Army Form C. 2118.

Place	Date	Hour	Summary of Events and Information	Remarks and references to Appendices
BOULEAUCOURT SECTOR	Feb. 21st		Enemy Artillery little activity during the day increase at night	
			Enemy M.G's slightly active at dusk on L.F. Brigade Front.	
			E.A. inactive during night	
	Feb. 23rd		Our Artillery very little activity shown	Strength
			M.G's usual harassing fire at night	O. O.Rs
			Aircraft inactive	10 177
			Enemy Artillery more active than previous day	Horses 36
			M.G's little activity shown at night	
			E.A. inactive	
	Feb. 24th		Our Artillery intermittent shelling throughout the day	
			M.G's usual harassing fire at night	
			Aircraft active all day	

WAR DIARY
or
INTELLIGENCE SUMMARY.

(Erase heading not required.)

Army Form C. 2118.

Place	Date	Hour	Summary of Events and Information	Remarks and references to Appendices
GUEUDECOURT SECTOR	Feb. 24th		Enemy Artillery more active than usual on Left Brigade front, intermittent shelling at night	
			M.G's active against Centre Brigade front	
			E.A. active at interval	
			No 2 Section relieved No 1 Section in the Right Brigade Sector relief complete 7.0 pm	
	Feb. 25th		Own Artillery active all day	
			M.G's usual harassing fire	
			Aircraft active at interval	
			Enemy Artillery increased activity shown	
			M.G's normal activity shown	
			E.A. inactive	

Army Form C. 2118.

WAR DIARY
or
INTELLIGENCE SUMMARY.
(Erase heading not required.)

Instructions regarding War Diaries and Intelligence Summaries are contained in F. S. Regs., Part II. and the Staff Manual respectively. Title pages will be prepared in manuscript.

XIX

Place	Date	Hour	Summary of Events and Information	Remarks and references to Appendices
GOUZEAUCOURT SECTOR	Feb 26th		Intelligence fairly active	
			Own Artillery usual harassing fire	
			M.G's fairly active	
			Aircraft	
			Enemy Artillery below normal	
			M.G's little activity shown	
			E.A. active	
	Feb 27th		Own Artillery usual activity shown during the day increasing at night	
			M.G's usual harassing fire at night	
			Aircraft fairly active	
			Enemy Artillery little activity shown	
			M.G's active at night	
			E.A. fairly active	

WAR DIARY
or
INTELLIGENCE SUMMARY.
(Erase heading not required.)

Army Form C. 2118.

Place	Date	Hour	Summary of Events and Information	Remarks and references to Appendices
BOUZEAUCOURT SECTOR	Feb 28th		Operation	
			118 Brigade carried out a raid on enemy trench objectives – enemy trenches from	
			R.32.a.15.78 ½ R.26.c.93.17	
			R.26.d.22.10 R.26.d.29.48	
			Four guns of 228 M.G. Coy cooperated by placing barrage at following points:	
			L.3 } Track & Trenches R.32.b.35.45	
			L.4 } R.32.b.45.60	
			L.7 } Trenches R.32.c.55.60 to	
			L.8 } R.32.c.28.28	
			Zero hour 5.15 a.m.	

R.B.M.C. Ken
Capt.
COMDG. No. 228 M.G. GUN COY.

www.ingramcontent.com/pod-product-compliance
Lightning Source LLC
Chambersburg PA
CBHW080829010526
44112CB00015B/2480